Head of the Family

Clayton C. Barbeau

Head of the Family

Christian Fatherhood
in the Modern World

SOPHIA INSTITUTE PRESS®
Manchester, New Hampshire

Head of the Family: Christian Fatherhood in the Modern World is a revised edition of *The Father of the Family: A Christian Perspective* (Huntington, Indiana: Our Sunday Visitor Publishing Division, 1990). This 2002 edition by Sophia Institute Press® does not include the foreword or the author's biography that appeared in the 1990 edition.

Printed in the United States of America

Cover design by Lorraine Bilodeau

Cover image, "On the Beach," courtesy of © Creatas.com

Sophia Institute Press®
Box 5284, Manchester, NH 03108
1-800-888-9344
www.sophiainstitute.com

Library of Congress Cataloging-in-Publication Data

Barbeau, Clayton C.
   Head of the family : Christian fatherhood in the modern
     world / Clayton C. Barbeau.
     p. cm.
   Rev. ed. of: The father of the family. 1990.
   Includes bibliographical references.
   ISBN 1-928832-77-6 (pbk. : alk. paper)
   1. Fathers — Religious life. 2. Fatherhood — Religious
     aspects — Catholic Church. I. Barbeau, Clayton C. Father
     of the family.
II. Title.
BX2352.5 .B37 2002
248.8'421 — dc21   2002151461

02 03 04 05 06 07 08 10 9 8 7 6 5 4 3 2 1

Contents

Introduction

Primitive peoples forged varied stories about their origins and the creation of the world. For some, the world was the result of a struggle between two deities, one of whom became enmeshed in matter. For others, the earth was formed out of raw matter by the arduous labor of the gods.

Today, some maintain that the universe and human life are the result of a chain of accidents — always presupposing, of course, an existing matter that could be involved in an accident. Standing tall and luminous above such perspectives is the first sentence of the Book of Genesis: "In the beginning God created the heavens and the earth."[1]

The purpose of Genesis is not to tell us how God created. In fact, there need be no contradiction between modern theories of evolution and the teaching of Genesis that God created everything that is. For Genesis neither asks nor answers the question as to how God created. It simply asserts that God created, and on this point the sacred author could not be clearer.

God fathers the universe into being

The first line of Genesis says that God created "the heavens and the earth." Not two or twenty, but one God. Not an accident,

[1] Gen. 1:1.

a collision in space, or another similar chance event, but simply God. There is just the calm statement that God "created the heavens and the earth."

As we read further in the creation story, we see that God, out of the fruitfulness of the divine being, created all that is, and all that God made was "good."

"So God created man in His own image, in the image of God He created him; male and female He created them. And God blessed them, and God said to them, 'Be fruitful and multiply, and fill the earth and subdue it; and have dominion over the fish of the sea and over the birds of the air and over every living thing that moves upon the earth.' "[2]

The Old Testament writers give us only hints as to the meaning of divine fatherhood. They see that God created the universe, "fathered" it, and continues to care for it. They recognize paternal solicitude in that act of the Lord for His first fallen creatures. "The Lord God made for Adam and for his wife garments of skins, and clothed them."[3]

Again and again, the image of the careful father is used to depict God's care for his creatures: "The Lord your God bore you, as a man bears his son";[4] "as a man disciplines his son, the Lord your God disciplines you."[5]

God fathers each one of us

Old Testament writers used language describing God's loving treatment as that of a father, but no writer before the time of

[2] Gen. 1:27-28.
[3] Gen. 3:21.
[4] Deut. 1:31.
[5] Deut. 8:5.

Christ dared to claim that our relationship to God was that of children to their loving father. Such a statement would have been impossible. From a Christian perspective, God's fatherhood is rooted not in creation, but in his loving intimacy with His Son. Only Jesus could truly say, "Abba, Father!"[6]

The first words attributed to Jesus appear in the Gospel of Luke, when Mary and Joseph find the boy Jesus in the Temple. "How is it that you sought me? Did you not know that I must be in my Father's house?"[7] In the Gospels, the name of the Father is constantly on Jesus' lips, in all His preaching, in the Sermon on the Mount, in His agony in the garden; and we who before His coming could not say "my Father," He taught to say "Our Father."[8]

St. Paul tells us that through Christ we are "all sons of God,"[9] and, moved by the spirit of our adoption, we can now cry, "Abba, 'Father!' " It is only through the Son that the fatherhood of God is extended to us; through Him the Father of the Word has become our Father. In John's Gospel, the risen Christ underscores this truth when He says to Mary of Magdala: "I am ascending to my Father and your Father, to my God and your God."[10]

The Jesus of the Fourth Gospel also makes it clear that our heavenly Father is to be approached through Christ: "I am the way and the truth and the life. No one comes to the Father except through me. If you know me, then you will also know my Father. From now on you do know Him and have seen Him."[11]

[6] Cf. Rom. 8:15.
[7] Luke 2:49.
[8] Cf. Matt. 6:9.
[9] Gal. 3:26.
[10] John 20:17.
[11] John 14:6.

Head of the Family

When Angelo Roncalli was cardinal patriarch of Venice, before he became Pope John XXIII, he said: "Jesus is the way. He is the supreme gift of the Father. For the Christian what matters is to be incorporated in Christ, and to be united to Him. The Son of God will make each baptized person a member of His Body, setting up a family relationship, that of a son, between Him and His heavenly Father. This way of expressing it was so dear to St. Paul that he used it 164 times in his letters."

God's fatherhood is made manifest, the future pope concluded, in the Church where, "In His Son, made man, the heavenly Father calls His creatures to life with Him as in a family."

True fatherhood is found in love and responsibility

The act of helping to conceive a new child — one of the greatest of a man's privileges — may make a man a biological father but not a true one. The mere breeding of young does not constitute true fatherhood. Military men serving in foreign lands have left behind them hundreds of thousands of children whom they have biologically fathered, but true fatherhood is not therein. So, too, with the unwed father who, even if aware of the consequences of his acts, accepts no responsibility for his child. This notion of responsibility is at the crux of true fatherhood.

The conscious sense of responsibility for the physical and spiritual well-being of others is the mark of a true father. It was in this sense that Joseph was the father of Jesus. Finding the boy Jesus in the temple, Mary says: "Your father and I have been looking for You with great anxiety."[12]

Thus, Joseph is a model for all who are true fathers, including those whose "children" they did not help to conceive biologically:

---

[12] Luke 2:48.

those who exert their energies, devote their time and efforts, and even endure "great anxiety" in guiding and caring for the young around them. Such men advise, assist, admonish, and deeply cherish all those who have need of them.

We have all had experience of such a person as this: the teacher to whom youngsters in trouble feel they can turn with a fuller confidence than they might have in their own fathers; the childless uncle who stands quietly in the background at family gatherings, but is never unaware of the needs of his nephews and nieces. Such men as these are true fathers, showing a love and a generosity free of any thought of reward: a true image, indeed, of the loving fatherhood of God.

Once we have recognized that true fatherhood is not necessarily allied with biological fatherhood, it is but a short step to the realization that all men are, by reason of their masculinity, called to be true fathers. The acceptance of responsibility for others, especially those too weak to stand alone, the solicitude for their spiritual and physical good rooted in a love devoid of selfishness: this fatherhood is the crown of manhood, the insignia of a man's maturity.

Sexuality is the holy foundation for fatherhood

Our concern here, however, is limited to a consideration of those of us who are fathers through biological conception or through adoption, and who are striving to become true fathers. Ours is a daily struggle to transform, with the grace of God, our biological or adoptive fatherhood into a real fatherhood of the heart and spirit, as well.

We must not misunderstand this emphasis upon a relationship in heart and spirit as superior to a relationship of a merely biological or legal/adoptive nature. The union of man and woman in sexual love is a union willed by God. It was God who created sexuality; it was God who chose in this fashion to give humankind a share in His own creative power and who ordained that sexual intercourse should be a source of intense pleasure and deep joy, a basic way for husband and wife to nourish their love for each other.

For those who may still think that there is something shameful and unworthy of God about sexual intimacy in marriage, we might recall the words of Pope John Paul II, who insists that "sexuality, by means of which man and woman give themselves to one another through the acts which are proper and exclusive to spouses, is by no means something purely biological, but concerns the innermost being of the human person as such."[13]

Human sexuality, along with everything else God created, is "very good."[14]

---

[13] *Familiaris Consortio*, no. 11.
[14] Gen. 1:31.

Head of the Family

Chapter 1

The Father as Creator

"[Parents] should realize that they are thereby cooperators with the love of God the Creator, and are, so to speak, the interpreters of that love. Thus they will fulfill their task with human and Christian responsibility, and, with docile reverence toward God, will make decisions by common counsel and effort. Let them thoughtfully take into account both their own welfare and that of their children, those already born and those which the future may bring. . . . Thus, trusting in divine Providence and refining the spirit of sacrifice, married Christians glorify the Creator and strive toward fulfillment in Christ when, with a generous human and Christian sense of responsibility, they acquit themselves of the duty to procreate."

Pastoral Constitution on the
Church in the Modern World, no. 60

The marriage vow is a creative vow in the fullest sense of that term. It is a vow that joins this man and this woman in a relationship meant to be stronger than any other, and, indeed, a true marriage is an indissoluble union. The union that is a true marriage is stronger even than the ties that bind parent and child. "Therefore a man leaves his father and mother and cleaves to his wife, and they become one flesh."[15] If a man's (or woman's) parents seek to prevent or undermine their child's marriage, that leaving of father and mother can be taken in its most severe sense.

Men and women must be free to marry or not to marry, but once their choice is freely made, once their pledge of fidelity is freely given, there is no return. Husband and wife are now "one body." Their union is — and has been since the creation of humankind — a union willed by God and cannot be broken by a merely human decision. No longer do husband and wife belong only to themselves, for they have vowed themselves to each other. They have promised to give themselves away, sexually and in all aspects of their life together. In words from St. Paul: "The wife does not rule over her own body, but the husband does; likewise the husband does not rule over his own body, but the wife does."[16]

[15] Gen. 2:24.
[16] 1 Cor. 7:4.

Like that other Christian paradox — that only the one who loses his life shall save it — this giving, too, reaps a rich return, for in giving themselves away, each gains the other. When this giving is done by two who are married "in the Lord,"[17] then it is Christ's own love that each gives and receives.

Spouses help complete and perfect each other

The indissolubility of marriage and the intimate union that exists in a sacramental marriage does not, of course, mean that marriage dissolves the personal identities of husband and wife. Their marriage vow is not a magic formula that wipes away all that marks them as unique persons. It does not replace their separate personalities with a neuter "we" that is neither the husband's nor the wife's personality. The "we" must indeed be created out of the love of each for the other, but the man and the woman must both work to create this "we." They must labor to bring into being this new personality, a personality that expresses their oneness, a personality that is larger and richer than that which either could know alone.

For man and woman help — by their complete dedication to the marriage and by their love — to bring each other to maturity. This is something that may be accomplished consciously or unconsciously, although too much self-consciousness about the transformation that is being worked out can be as harmful as being totally unaware that such a transformation is meant to come about.

What both husband and wife must know is that their life together will be one long creative endeavor to fulfill the other, to unfold tenderly in the other all of the good that the lover has seen there, to let it nourish in an atmosphere of love and appreciation.

[17] 1 Cor. 7:39.

What too often happens is quite the reverse. Each party comes to the marriage radiant with the belief that this other person is going to heal all of his physical and mental aches and pains and is quite surprised to discover, not too much later, that the other has aches and pains of his own. This leads to disillusionment, to bitterness, the feeling that one has been unfairly "trapped" by sexual desire or the wiles of the other person, often followed by recriminations, arguments, or embittered silence and the bearing of a sometimes lifelong grudge.

Love expresses itself in symbols

How different the marriage that is founded upon a true love for the other, a constant desire to protect and feed and keep healthy the happiness of the other. Such a marriage cannot become the vicious snake of disillusion eating its own bitter tail of dissatisfaction. Such a marriage rooted in mutual love becomes a creation of marvelous beauty, with each party seeking new ways of expressing the love and happiness he or she knows.

Every sort of symbolism comes into play here, and the world becomes rich with unexpected surprises. The canvas of marriage becomes glorious with one shared experience following another; each tries to outdo the other in finding new ways to express his love. The early verbalizing, the magic and romantic lyricism of love letters, and long, late-night telephone conversations — all of these are left behind. Even the constant repetition of the words of love finds husband and wife admitting to each other that words do not express what they wish them to express.

Thus, verbal symbols give way to a thousand variations of concrete symbols: a surprise gift, a note on the refrigerator, an evening planned totally for the other — always designed to unlock in the other that secret closet of joy. In creating their masterpiece, truly "their life's work," husband and wife each look to the other's needs. Each seeks to understand the other person, to meet and respond to the call of the other at each given moment.

For the man this demands a knowledge not only of what it is he has married — a woman — but of whom he has married: this very personal, unique woman. Thus, the husband must drop his easy assumptions and superficial estimates of "women" and truly seek to understand and love this particular woman.

Marriage, then, is a creative work. Both parties must labor to make a beautiful marriage. The wreckage of the miserable marriages we see all about us today is due mainly to this: that one or the other or both parties did not know — or did not have the maturity or psychological freedom to act upon this knowledge — that to make a marriage work means to work at making a marriage.

Often enough, if only one party is willing or able to work, to continue to sacrifice, the marriage can at least be rescued from disaster, if not transformed. The advice of the first letter of Peter to the wives of pagan husbands fits equally well the circumstances of husbands whose wives are less than Christian: "Some, though they do not obey the word, may be won without word by the behavior of their wives, when they see your reverent and chaste behavior."[18]

Sex: the ultimate symbol of love

In the communion of marital love, sexual intercourse is at once the most beautiful and the most underrated of communications — underrated because, while our society is full of throbbing eroticism, there is hardly any knowledge or appreciation of the meaning and purpose of sex. To see sex as mere thrill or pleasure, even as the

---

[18] 1 Pet. 3:1-2.

highest pleasure, is to underestimate sex. Of all the means of communicating love that are open to husband and wife, "making love" is the most perfect. For either party to seek from it only personal satisfaction is to destroy the richest symbol of mutual love that husband and wife can have.

The man who peeled the banana, ate the skin, and threw the banana away was always good for a laugh in old-time vaudeville shows, and yet he was doing only what the sexual thrill-seeker is doing.

The real substance of the marriage act is the mutual love it expresses. That is what is so tragic about all of the books on sex so easily available today. No amount of "technique" or "sexual performance" can enrich sexual intercourse that is not first an act of love. On the contrary, a mutual love and a mutual desire to bring and give to the other's whole person will bring about gestures, caresses, and other expressions of love so rich and so unselfconscious that one could only degrade them by calling them a "technique." Husband and wife assume an equal responsibility for making sexual intercourse satisfying for both. While the husband's inclination seems to orient him toward "rapid conquest," he should remember that a woman's inclination often craves assurances of his tender and constant love prior to the actual beginning of sexual intercourse.

Someone has said that men make love from the outside in, while women make love from the inside out, and there is some truth to this idea. It simply means that, in general, men begin with physical arousal and build inward toward emotional feelings, while women tend to become emotionally aroused first, then build toward physical arousal. The trick is for husband and wife to try lovingly to keep in mind "where the other is at" during the love-making process.

When husband and wife succeed in this, love-making does just that: it makes more love. Sexual intercourse becomes the positive, dynamic symbol of the interpenetration of their lives and personalities. It is a major symbol, but not the only one. Making love is part of the continent of their life together, not an island separated from their daily lives.

We become co-creators with God through love

We shall discuss in future pages the even greater symbolism of the sexual union in marriage, but here we are restricting ourselves to the creative element in marriage and family life. Procreation means to create on behalf of. Men and women are allowed to create on behalf of God. The children born to mothers and fathers are meant for eternal life. Sexual intercourse is thus the ultimate creative act of men and women. By it, they are allowed to create human persons destined for resurrection and eternity. All of Michelangelo's creations (the frescoes in the Sistine Chapel, the dome of St. Peter's basilica, the great works of sculpture for Pope Julius's tomb), all of the magnificent outpourings of a creative genius are not worth one baby. And Michelangelo could not alone produce a baby.

If the love of a man and woman that expresses itself in the creation of a hundred symbols of love is to express itself in a child, God (and the healthy reproductive systems of a man and woman) must be there. Fatherhood is impossible without the direct involvement of God.

It is only by God's divine act that an embodied soul comes into being through the union of the sperm and ovum of the parents. It is only by God's creative act that a new human person will result from the physical and spiritual act of the parents, a person of intelligence and will, reflecting God's own image and destined for eternal life with Him. The psalmist sings, "When You send forth Your Spirit, they are created, and You renew the face of the earth."[19]

If a couple's love is to be fruitful, if they are to incarnate their love in a completely new person, then their love must be a love in relationship with God. The Creator must bend to them, as it were, and breathe the "breath of life" into their joined sperm and ovum.

Sexual communion renews
the sacrament of Matrimony

The sexual intercourse of husband and wife, every time they make love, is a word uttered into the night, a prayer that God bless this union with the word that is the "breath of life," indeed, life itself — whether a child is conceived or not. The union of husband and wife, which is a union in Christ, is a form of worship — and some theologians suggest that when spouses make love, they celebrate the sacrament of their marriage. In giving themselves to each other in the sacrament of their marriage, they give themselves not only to each other, but to Christ. The Rite of Matrimony used prior to the Second Vatican Council, until the mid-1960s, recognized this fact with the phrase "With my body I thee worship."

Even when a particular act of making love does not result in the conception of a child — and most of the time it does not — sexual intercourse is yet immeasurably richer than any mere thrill-seeker can imagine. In a truly Christian marriage, sexual intercourse is a symbolizing that communicates God's self-gift, or grace. By making love, husband and wife nourish their relationship with each other and with God.

[19] Cf. Ps. 104:30.

The tremendous paradox of marriage is this: the most bodily expression of love is also the most spiritual expression of love.

Having chosen to live within the sacrament of marriage, a husband and wife choose to live not only intimately with each other, but in intimacy with God. One of the richest springs of this divine life for each other will be sexual intercourse; their bodily and spiritual union is the living out of their specific holiness; and Christian holiness is growth in a specific sacramental role, which is part of the larger drama that is the life of the Church.

Sexual love is creative and salvific

Sexual intimacy, therefore, is not only the source of new human life and deepening marital love; it is meant to be a source of that "more abundant life,"[20] of growth in the divine love-life. In its *Pastoral Constitution on the Church in the Modern World*, no. 48, Vatican II stated: "Authentic married love is caught up into divine love and is directed and enriched by the redemptive power of Christ and the salvific action of the Church, with the result that the spouses are effectively led to God and are helped and strengthened in their lofty role as fathers and mothers."

The commitment husband and wife make to one another, then, is creative. It is the necessary condition for the full flowering of their love life. It permits them experiences of a quality impossible to those who do not enjoy the freedom that flows from the vows of Christian marriage — notably, couples who merely "live together" — including the openness that can spring from an unquestioned fidelity to the other.

Even as those who have grounded their marriage in this sacred territory are open to each other, so do they strive to remain open

[20] Cf. John 10:10.

to others — especially to the children of their love. Such people know what the psalmist felt when he sang: "Your wife will be like a fruitful vine within your house; your children will be like olive shoots around your table."[21]

The true father sees himself neither as tied down by his children nor as one ensnared by forces beyond his control; rather, he sees himself as a man the Lord would use to enrich creation further. He sees himself as one through whom the almighty Creator has chosen to work, and he sees his children as mysteries — persons willed by God to fulfill a place not to be decided by the father, but by and through the grace of God.

Only God can create out of nothing. Only God can cause something to exist by a mere act of His will. For human beings, even in their "garden of delights," it would have been necessary that they have something to work on or with if they were to make something new. Thus, if a man were to make a vase, he must have clay to shape. If he intends to carve a lyre, he must have wood to whittle and a knife to cut with. Yet God gave to humankind a share in the divine creativity, a higher share than any other creature. God gave people the power to bring into existence new persons, which the Spirit would quicken into life both physically and spiritually.

This is the closest that humankind can come to the creativity of God, to share in God's creative activity in this way. It is the great blessing of God upon us — and even if it is mitigated by our fallen nature, it remains a blessing still.

Women sense the mystery of creation instinctively

In Genesis, even with the Garden of Eden a thing of the past, Eve sings a song of joy at the birth of Cain, her first child: "I have

---

[21] Ps. 128:3.

gotten a man with the help of the Lord."[22] And in John's Gospel, Jesus says: "When a woman is in travail she has sorrow, because her hour has come; but when she is delivered of the child, she no longer remembers the anguish, for joy that a child is born into the world."[23]

It is in the womb of woman that human beings are fashioned. Her role results in profound physical, emotional, and spiritual processes that work slowly at the very core of her life as a woman. The basic cycle of her physical life changes; her breasts grow tender, the child in her womb draws from her body its sustenance, grows larger, and moves about. She bears within her the incalculable treasure, patiently awaiting the "fullness of time." Her close contact with the mystery is full of a meaning she cannot utter. At the center of her being is a rich pool of silence, the silence of contemplative communion — reverent and joyful at one moment, anxious and uncertain the next. It is a silence akin to the silence of Heaven when the seventh seal was opened,[24] for the seal of a new life has opened within her, and the vision cannot be uttered.

The father has no such experience of his fatherhood. Indeed, the unique act whereby he cooperated in the conception of this particular child may be lost for him in the past. It may take an effort for him to grasp his responsibility for the transformations taking place in his spouse. Rarely will his sense of fatherhood blossom fully within him prior to the birth of the child, before the baby is free of the mother and visibly belonging to both of them. Even then his recognition of his parenthood will be a gradual enlightenment. In our time, fortunately, many men choose to be present for

[22] Gen. 4:1.

[23] John 16:21.

[24] Cf. Rev. 6:1–7:8.

the birth of their child, and this helps a great deal to begin what is called the "bonding process" between father and infant.

The mother, in most cases, continues to play a unique role in the child's life, especially when most women today wisely choose to breast-feed their newborns. But fathers play an increasingly active role in caring for and raising their children, and the father is best advised to take advantage of every opportunity to maximize his involvement in his child's life, beginning at the moment of birth. The man who willingly abdicates the care of his infant child entirely to his wife is making a mistake, and his life is greatly impoverished.

Children add a deep new dimension to marriage

After the birth of the first child, a man's relationship with his wife becomes richer than when he was only her husband; he is now the father of their child. She is now a mother, and in the first months of her new motherhood, she will have need of him in ways different from before. New depths of tenderness and solicitude that he called forth out of her must now be met by an equal tenderness and solicitude on his part. He has helped to call forth a new woman, a mother — and now she calls forth a new man, a father.

Theirs is no longer only the relationship of husband and wife, for their mutual love has been blessed by God and is now embodied in a new person, the person of their child. Each has given to the other the image of their love. The ineffable, unutterable feelings each had tried falteringly to communicate to the other — and never adequately expressed — are now embodied. The child is, among other imponderables, the personification of their love.

The family symbolizes the mystery of the Trinity

This would be mystery enough, even if it were all. For who can comprehend how the mutual love of a man and woman could became incarnated? But this is not all. The mystery is a symbol of the greatest of mysteries: the mystery of the inner life of God. For in every human family we have only feeble images of the Trinity. God the Father from all eternity has generated the Son, and the mingling of their mutual love is the Holy Spirit. The Father is truly the Father, the Son is truly the Son; theirs is indeed a relationship of paternity and filiation, a relationship that is the ground out of which all created relationships of fatherhood and sonship spring. "For this reason," says the letter to the Ephesians, "I bow my knees before the Father, from whom every family in Heaven and on earth is named."[25]

To share in God's own creation of new life is the greatest blessing of all — a privilege even the angels do not enjoy — and yet this does not end the creative activity required of husband and wife. Indeed, it is only the beginning, and this is why adoptive parents truly are the parents of their child in the fullest sense of the word. Parents, biological or adoptive, begin a new endeavor: they must set about to build a temple for this new image of God; they must give a home to the child.

Home life reflects divine life

Even as God's creation reflects the divine image, so our homes will image us. We are all familiar with homes where the overflow of love is like a warm hearth. As one Italian lady said to a prospective tenant looking at a large flat with only one heater: "Ah, but a large family warms a house." We are also familiar with the sterile chill of those homes where a mutual distrust, a certain fear of one another and of life itself, has led to a cold-bloodedness that is like a constant draft from some dark cellar.

[25] Eph. 3:14.

The home, the home life, the family itself will reflect the spirit and love-artistry of both husband and wife; but, before God, it is husband and wife who will be held responsible for this whole creation, and in a special way this is true for the husband and father. It is sad but true: many a man, through thoughtlessness and insensitivity, squelches his wife's inclinations toward warmth, creativity, and faith, and the result is a home that is unpleasant to live in.

Christian home life requires stability

It is always salutary for the fathers of families to recall that, in the creation story in Genesis, it is Eve who first eats of the fruit — and absolutely nothing happens. But when Adam chooses to take a bite — when, in effect, the two act together as a couple — well, we are all too aware of the consequences of that pathetic act. In creating the home, we should keep in mind that ideally the family home is just that: a family home. It should be stable, solid; a home must be somewhere before it can be something. Stable people are the products of stable homes. The person "at home" in the world is generally the one who has a home in the world. Today some men endanger their marriages, the destinies of their children, and the happiness of their families by accepting as a "fact of life" — if they want to "succeed" — the need for constant transfers, for movement hither and yon.

"Success" for the Christian must be measured in terms other than those of the modern corporation. A man does not sacrifice the greater for the less.

This creation of the home life that seems to demand the stability of a home is the concern of both father and mother. It is they who must decide where the family shall live and how they are to provide for it. Compromises will often be necessary in this matter, since we must live in this society. Only the father and mother will know what was a necessary compromise and what was a cop-out to the social drift.

When the home, for some fundamental reason, lacks that stability, the parents must strive even harder to make the family itself an anchor for their children. So long as the life within is stable, ordered full of mutual love and respect — a true family life — the home could be a flat, a tent. All the wandering tribes of the past and present have this sort of stability, this strong family loyalty.

Family life of such substance is not accidental. It does not merely happen as children are born, but must be consciously worked at by the parents. Again, it is a creation in the fullest sense. The family is a work of art, a mosaic of the mutual love and respect of husband, wife, and children, a mosaic illumined by the One who called Himself "the light of the world."[26]

In a unique way, then, and in cooperation with his wife, the father of the family is one who is and knows himself to be responsible for creation and, in many ways, is himself a creator. But he must never forget that it is only in Christ and through Christ that any creation at all is possible: "All things were made through Him, and without Him was not anything made that was made."[27]

[26] John 8:12.
[27] John 1:3.

Chapter 2

The Father as Lover

"When there is [a] question of harmonizing conjugal love with the responsible transmission of life, the moral aspect of any procedure does not depend solely on sincere intentions or on an evaluation of motives, but must be determined by objective standards. These, based on the nature of the human person and his acts, preserve the full sense of mutual self-giving and human procreation in the context of true love. Such a goal cannot be achieved unless the virtue of conjugal chastity is sincerely practiced. . . . All should be persuaded that human life and the task of transmitting it are not realities bound up with this world alone. Hence they cannot be measured or perceived only in terms of it, but always have a bearing on the eternal destiny of men."

Pastoral Constitution on the
Church in the Modern World, no. 51

M arriage, to be sure, is not instituted solely for procreation; rather, its very nature as an unbreakable compact between persons, and the welfare of the children, both demand that the mutual love of the spouses be embodied in a rightly ordered manner, that it grow and ripen. Therefore, marriage persists as a whole manner and communion of life, and maintains its value and indissolubility, even when, despite the often intense desire of the couple, offspring are lacking."[28]

In Matthew's Gospel, Jesus says: "You shall love your neighbor as yourself."[29] St. Paul tells us that this commandment is "the fulfilling of the law."[30]

"As yourself": how aware we are of ourselves! Our own feelings, hopes, fears, memories, troubles, and joys are constantly with us, thrusting themselves like barricades between our deepest selves and others. We are always on the lookout to protect our interests, to care for our persons, our reputations, to protect our property. Above all, we are always quick to make excuses for our blunders, to give the best possible interpretations for our actions, to blame others for our mistakes.

---

[28] *Pastoral Constitution on the Church in the Modern World*, no. 50.

[29] Matt. 22:39.

[30] Rom. 13:10.

"From my point of view" and "But you've got to understand my position" are phrases often on our lips. No one, not even the murderer or the one who commits suicide, means to will himself evil. The murderer sees his crime as benefitting himself somehow, and the one who commits suicide sees death as a good opposed to some evil that appears to be greater. We will our own good — that is part of our nature.

The best definition of love

But what is love?

Ultimately, love is a mystery, and an all-encompassing definition is impossible. St. Thomas Aquinas,[31] however, offers us the best working definition, and when he tells us that to love is to will the good of the other, he is echoing Jesus' own words. This definition includes two important points that require elaboration. The first of these is that love pertains not so much to the emotions or the sexual appetite as to the will.

It is the will, informed by the intellect, that chooses to love or not to love. True love between a man and a woman rules out neither the physical nor the emotional, but subordinates these faculties to human judgment and will. Only the clear realization that love is a matter of the will can help us avert the tragedy that follows the belief that love is solely a matter of the emotions or of sexual desire. Actually, sexual and emotional attachments are deepened and strengthened with the passage of time if there is true love.

The contemporary insanity about sex, marriage, and family life, the personal misery of millions of our fellow human beings, are consequences of giving the wrong answer to the question

---

[31] St. Thomas Aquinas (c. 1225-1274), Dominican philosopher, theologian, and Doctor.

"What is love?" There is a rather widespread belief that love is the desire for sexual union with another person. We have partially indicated in the previous chapter that love and sexual passion are not the same when we pointed out that sexual intercourse is but one method of communicating love. Trying to found love on sexual desire alone is like trying to plant a tree on the surface of a raging sea.

Love means more than desire or excitement

If love depends upon sexual desire, it is doomed to die when sexual desire fades away — and illness or accident can wipe away in a moment the basis of that desire. Most certainly the strongest of passionate desires is diminished when the desired object is attained and each day becomes more familiar — unless love is present.

Is it too much of an oversimplification to say that the divorce courts are full of people who married thinking that the sexual excitement aroused by the other was love and who, after a couple of years of marriage, have caused that sexual passion to subside, have convinced themselves that their love has died? One woman, after her fourteenth divorce, announced she was still seeking the "right man." She cannot find him because no human being can keep sexual passion alive while at the same time satisfying it.

More prevalent than the confusion of love with physical desire is the notion that love is an irresistible emotional force against which a human being cannot stand. According to the simplifications of our contemporary folklore, especially of our literature and entertainment media, love is liable to strike us at any moment like a crippling disease — given the virus of the right object. Those screen lovers who wail: "I can't help myself" or, "There's nothing I can do," and, alas, those influenced by them, would make of love such a sickness.

To say that this emotional state is love, however, is to identify love with something in our nature even more unpredictable than sexual desire. Our emotional states vary from day to day; hour to hour, our moods change — our cheerfulness today may give way to tomorrow's sadness. No one laughs all day and, equally, no one could long sustain the high-pitched emotional frenzy that some would tell us constitutes love.

As an act of the will, love requires freedom

These two errors about love — that it is sexual desire or an emotional state or a combination of the two — both make the same mistake of explaining love in terms of what it does to the individual who feels the emotion or knows the passion; they look inward to the lover and not outward to the person loved. Further, they would place love outside the control of the person loving and, in so doing, rob it of its most precious attribute. The very reason love is priceless is because it is free.

That love which is not freely given is not love at all. Nothing can force us to love another person. God does not force us to love Him. Love is totally under our control. If it were not, Jesus could not have commanded us to love, for He would have been commanding us to do something beyond our power.

Yet, Jesus did command us to love, and in a certain way: "You shall love your neighbor as yourself." When the free choice of our will to unite our life with another person expresses itself in a vow of lifelong fidelity and is further protected by daily rededication to dependence upon God alone, this free choice is capable of weathering all the storms of time and circumstance. Such a love can withstand even the emotional or sexual attraction of another who might seem to promise us more in return for our love. Even if our present condition is miserable and a change of spouses seems to offer immense advantages, we have but to look to Jesus, who died a miserable death on the Cross in order to know what love can demand.

Love does not seek a return

"To will the good of the other." There is no hint here of any return to the lover. That is what we mean when we say that love is ecstatic — that all flows out to the other. True, we do in actual fact often seek a return of love, often seek a reward; but to the degree that this is so, there is a dilution of the purity of the love; and if ever our love craves only possession of the beloved, it has given way to lust.

If we want the good of the other only because that good will redound to our own benefit, our love has become covetousness. Both of these falsifications of love result in a depersonalization of the beloved. We strip the beloved of her subjectivity; we no longer see her as a person, but instead look upon her simply as some object having reference only to ourselves. We begin to look upon her as important because of that relationship she has to us, some use we might put her to, rather than as one who is precious and unique and to be loved for what she is in herself.

Love allows others to be "present" for us

Gabriel Marcel, the twentieth-century French philosopher, is especially rich in insights into the problems of our age. Like many other writers, theologians, and psychologists, Marcel speaks of the need for us to strive to allow others to be "present" for us in such a way that we see these others not in relationship to ourselves or for some use we might put them to, but as they see themselves. Marcel uses the term *presence* when speaking of this, of our being present for others, of others being present for us.

Head of the Family

The great Jewish philosopher Martin Buber had a crucial experience that radically changed his outlook upon the world, an experience that gives us an indication of what this sort of presence entails. One day a young man came to Buber with a few questions. The philosopher was polite, neither more nor less friendly than he would have been with any other of his students, and the young man departed. Shortly after leaving, the young man committed suicide.

The news of the death made Buber profoundly aware of the fact that his visitor had not been really "present" for him during the interview. He, Buber, had been courteous enough, had answered the student's questions patiently, but had failed to take enough interest in his visitor to see him as a person, to see that the young man was troubled by larger, unasked questions. Buber later learned that it was those very unasked questions that the young man had hoped would be answered. Buber had been the student's last resort, and Buber had failed.

A clipping on my desk from a recent newspaper gives another example of the turning of a person into an object. A young man called his psychoanalyst to inform him that he had slashed his wrists in an attempt at suicide and to beg the psychoanalyst to come by and see him. The doctor replied that it "would not be good professional conduct to see a patient under such circumstances" and told the young man to go get first aid and come to his office for an appointment the next day.

This young man, like Buber's student, succeeded in committing suicide. Whether or not it would have been good professional conduct, might it not have been good human conduct to have gone to the aid of the young man? The fact that a man is a "patient" or "client" should not make us forget that he is, first of all, a human being.

Depersonalization leads to boredom — or tragedy

All of us can profit by these examples. How often in our own home life do we not tend to look upon our wives and our children as objects — "the wife," "the kids" — rather than as unique beings, each possessed of his or her own inviolate personality?

Often we do not realize that we have turned them into objects until some crisis arises, some tragedy jolts us awake, making us realize that we do not own this other person: that he or she is capable of being lost to us, that he or she has hidden depths that we shall never know, that he or she can suffer while we can do little about it.

How often do we tend really to care for another, to be "carefull" about another, to "will the good of the other" — in short, to love another — only when some such crisis as sickness or accident has jolted us awake?

In some homes the crisis is not sickness or accident but a result of the revolt of a human spirit against such depersonalization. Some years ago, a young girl, described as a good student and a normal youngster, sat in the front room of her home with a loaded .22-caliber rifle on her lap. When her fourteen-year-old brother entered the house, she shot him dead. Her mother was at work, and so was her father. She sat down to await their arrival so that she might kill them before killing herself. When her mother came up the path, she panicked and gave up her scheme.

Questioned, this girl gave as her motive for the crime the fact that everything was so "dull." Her mother and her father went off to work in the morning while she and her brother went to school; they all came home in the evening, ate their evening meal, watched a little TV, and went to bed in order to wake up the next morning and start the same routine over again. If that was life, she felt, let's have done with it.

This child's reaction was tragically drastic, but was not her situation similar to that in millions of homes in our land? Is not this, basically, the reason hundreds of thousands of our young people are looking for "thrills" by turning to drugs, alcohol, and premature sexual activity? There are other reasons, but they are subsidiary reasons really, for all reasons lead back to the home.

Families are hungry for the father's love

In the home from which teenage drug abuse stems, we often discover a state of anarchy, because the home is without enough parental involvement, perhaps due to divorce or mere abdication in favor of the pursuit of a more and more affluent lifestyle. In such homes, we find a situation where the sense of adventure is dead for another reason: because love is dead.

Why did the girl who killed her brother not feel free to discuss with her parents how she felt about the way she lived? Why did she not feel that life itself was worth living? Perhaps the fact that she seldom saw her father and her mother except in front of the TV set is one reason. Accepting her description as accurate, she was living in a house filled with strangers who were not "present" to her, people between whom apparently flowed no communication of loving care or even interest in one another.

As Christians, we know the entire message of Christ to be summed up in one word: *love*. To be a Christian means to love. What the girl was hungry for — what she knew only as a great lack, a boredom — was love. What all the sad faces at the stop lights, all the hypochondriacs in the doctors' offices, all the tragic figures shooting heroin or sniffing cocaine, all the steady drinkers near the bar needed a long time ago was love.

If our homes are not centers of Christian love, how can we expect our society to know the effects of that love? As the fathers of families, we must be lovers. We must will the good of all those under our care. We must look constantly for their perfection, recognizing that they, even the tiniest infants, have an absolute equality with us as persons.

Family headship demands service and tenderness

Our authority as parents in our homes must always be used to achieve the highest possible good for those under our care. We do not use our authority for our own good — such is, indeed, the basic misuse — but for the temporal and eternal good that we will for those we love. The man who does not see his authority as essentially a means whereby he serves those for whom he is responsible neither knows what authority is nor deserves to have it. The service of the father is a service rooted in a love that will show itself in his constant effort to help toward maturity and independence the children under his care.

The love of a husband for his wife is a profound commitment to her good. That love is limitless, the father soon discovers, as it opens outward to the children born of his love for his wife. The child must be recognized not merely as the incarnation of the mutual love of the parents, but as a person, a body-soul unity having an intellect and a will and a destiny that is greater than merely symbolizing their union. And this child in his earliest years will know only one thing: whether or not he is loved. The child will not be capable of any concrete return of that love for months, and yet from his first hours, the child craves the experience of love.

This experience — which flows into the baby's consciousness with the very milk he drinks, the air he breathes, the way he is handled — is crucial to the infant. Doctors, psychologists, and educators today insist upon the fact that the healthy child physically and mentally is the child secure in the love of his parents. Not the finest of medical attention can compensate for the child's lack of love.

The child's need for love makes itself known through his demands for attention. To give attention is to show a sign of love. Desire for attention is but another way of saying that the child wants you to let him be "present" for you. But the child's demands for attention will diminish as soon as he "proves" to his satisfaction that he is loved. Here is another case where "love casts out fear,"[32] for the child's first thrusting out into the world is a traumatic experience, and only a solid cushion of love can counteract the shock. That the child's overt demands for attention diminish should not mean that we pay less attention to him, that we cease to let the child be "present" for us or to let ourselves be "present" for him. The child has need of a loving, attentive father for all the years of his growth.

Modern distractions compete for our attention

Attention. Both the advertising and entertainment industries are entirely devoted to the pursuit and capture of our attention. Each day we enter a world full of the confused noise and colors of those frantically clamoring for our attention in order to sell us something — often something we not only do not need, but would be better off without.

This constant din of the professional attention-getters defeats its own purpose; unable to pay attention to all at once, most people have ceased to pay attention to any. Television, of course, frequently subverts even this defensive reaction on our part by inducing a drug-like stupor that keeps our eyes focused on the screen through endless commercials.

[32] 1 John 4:18.

The Father as Lover

Advertising is everywhere, and our natural inclination is to become calloused to even the most blatant sales appeals. To do otherwise would drive us mad. Even in those areas where attention is required of us, it has become exceedingly difficult. Magazine articles are sandwiched between advertisements; television-network executives admit openly that the purpose of television is to deliver an audience to advertisers; classroom lectures are interrupted by the sound of jets overhead; heavy traffic is made the more dangerous by highway billboards or neon signs.

The modern world makes it more and more difficult for us to give our undivided attention even when we wish to do so. Yet, one of the ways in which we evidence our love for others is by paying attention to them, by allowing them to be "present" for us. After all, a person is not an advertisement.

A human being in need of us, if only as a listener, does not announce that need in neon lights, does not dramatize that need through the medium of an eye-catching advertisement or through the breathless voice of an announcer. Some human beings have, indeed, been driven to extremities in order to focus our attention on their plight: the man who slashed his wrists was one such, and even that failed him. But most struggle to maintain a surface calm even when they are inwardly agonizing.

"Those who are unhappy," Simone Weil wrote, "have no need for anything in this world but people capable of giving them their attention." In order to give others this attention which is their greatest need, we must look upon them not as "wife," "child," "patient," "client," or "business acquaintance," but as "myself." That this is difficult no one denies. Simone Weil calls it a "miracle," but if it is a miracle, it is a miracle of grace. Christ, who commanded us to do it, will not withhold from us the grace necessary to fulfill His command.

Jesus is our model for true attentiveness

We ought, however, to be careful of mistaking a sentry-like watching for this attentiveness, especially in the case of our children. To be overly conscious of everything the child does, to be constantly fearful of the infant's every move, always on the watch to warn and interrupt, is to render the child totally insecure. Such a persistent hounding is the farthest thing from true attentiveness that can be imagined, and it can do untold psychological damage to the child.

No, true attentiveness is that which allows the child to be present as the child is at the moment, to accept and love him without qualification, and, through that acceptance and love, to provide the child with the security in which he can grow free from fear or nagging harassment.

"Fear not for I am with you"; "Do not be afraid": How often these words appear in Scripture. It was into a frightened and utterly hopeless world that Christ was born. Love came to drive out fear and hatred and violence.

It is significant to note how many of His miracles involved some personal contact between Jesus and the person on whom the miracle was performed: the blind man felt Jesus' fingers apply the moistened earth; the sick felt the touch of his hand. Everywhere His love was expressed in that sort of personal relationship, a very human relationship.

Jesus' disciples, whom He loved, went out without fear or hatred and told others the Good News. They had no guns or bombs, no television or computerized printing presses; the world was not changed by such things as these, but by the love these people had for Jesus and for their fellow human beings. It was a personal love that they proclaimed — and it is a personal love that we are called upon to practice.

We must love the little "enemies" in our home

Yet Christ calls us to more than just the love of our neighbors: "But I say to you, love your enemies, and pray for those who persecute you, that you may be sons of your Father who is in Heaven. . . . For if you love those who love you, what reward have you? Do not even the tax collectors do the same? And if you salute only your brethren, what more are you doing than others? Do not even the Gentiles do the same? You, therefore, must be perfect, as your heavenly Father is perfect."[33]

It is easy to love our neighbor, even our enemy, in the abstract, but it becomes more difficult when he lives with us. What is our child when he is interfering with our conversation, tearing up our magazines, or racing through the living room, but the particular little "enemy" we are called upon to love at that moment? If our love is not to stop within the confines of our home, or even at the periphery of our circle of friends, it must begin at home.

How can we expect to love those who hate us if we do not know even how to love those who live under our very roofs and who love us? On the other hand, love, once we have recognized it and disciplined ourselves to its practice, will diffuse itself; it cannot be contained. The man who has learned to love his children when they are his "enemies" has made the first step toward loving strangers who are his enemies.

Attentive love is a daily martyrdom

The fact that love calls for the sacrifice of self should come as no surprise. Hard though it may be to accept in an era dedicated to self-gratification and the pursuit of comfort, the essence of love is sacrifice. We have the constant reminder of Christ's Cross that it

[33] Matt. 5:44, 46-48.

is through sacrifice that love is proved. "By this we know love, that He laid down His life for us; and we ought to lay down our lives for the brethren."[34]

No love worthy of the name can stop at words: it will express itself in action. If to love is to will the good of the other, then the ultimate in love is to offer up the greatest good we ourselves possess, our own lives, for the good of the other. Let us not make the mistake of thinking that this offering up of our lives must take the form of martyrdom on the battlefield or a heroic moment during a shipwreck; it is a sacrifice that we who are married are called to make every day.

At the time of our wedding, we dedicated ourselves to giving our lives for the good of the one we love. Our heroic moments occur day in and day out — whenever we have to deny ourselves for others. The lifelong sacrifice of ourselves to the good of others is what constitutes our fatherhood in its fullness. It would be worthwhile for us to examine our consciences regularly to see whether we are fulfilling that promise. How often lately have we taken back the gift of ourselves that we offered before God on our wedding day? If we have allowed "business" and the world to make us forget it, we have called back the sacrifice; we have recanted at the stake. What was meant to be our martyrdom and our triumph has become our treason and our defeat.

The struggle to love unconditionally

It is hard to love even when that love is returned. Even the best will in the world cannot, at times, overcome all fatigue, cannot restrain the momentary sharpness of the tongue or the quickness to respond to one hurt by another.

[34] 1 John 3:16.

The ego, when hurt, would sulk, licking its wounds and snapping at those who approach. Pride will rear its head angrily. Humiliation will desire the luxury of self-pity. Failure will seek a scapegoat upon whom the guilt can be lashed. More often than not, the wounded ego, the stung pride, the sense of failure will be due to some event that occurred outside the home — at the job, or in the course of the day's activities — and the temptation will be strong to bring these hurts home, to make others suffer for what we have suffered.

To assent to this is to open the gates of the family to the enemy of love. When our love is not returned, or is not returned in the way we think it should be, the temptation is even stronger. At such times we must remember that the call to love is not a call conditioned by an expectation of return. Our love for others is to be patterned after the love of Him who "first loved us."[35] And the pattern of Christ's love is the Cross, the humiliation, the agony, the death that He suffered for our sake. The Cross, a sign of failure for the nonbeliever, is for the Christian the sign of love. Christ, the Bridegroom, gave life to His Bride, the Church, by His death on the Cross.

A father's love unites him to Christ

A father cannot expect either his marriage or his family to survive if he forgets that his greatest obligation is one that he shares with all Christians: the obligation to love. To the degree that he loves without thought of return, to the extent that he looks upon even his enemy as infinitely precious in the sight of God, and therefore infinitely worthy of his own attention and care, he is loving that person, however weakly, as God loves him.

[35] 1 John 4:19.

When a man's love for another leads him to the exchange of the vows of the sacrament of marriage, his love is caught up into the supernatural, and he truly gives and receives a love transfigured by the love of Christ. United in the love of Christ, husband and wife, living and loving in the sacrament they share, will find that their sacrificial love, like all true sacrifice, will be rendered fruitful by God: it will bear new life. Having given up their lives in Christ, they will have life more abundantly. "For . . . whoever loses his life for my sake will find it."[36]

A couple may have children and, thus, more readily see that love *is* life; but should a couple find themselves unable to conceive and give birth to children, still their marriage can be fruitful. Their shared love in Christ becomes a shared life in Christ, the means to their mutual growth in holiness, the preparation for that ultimate life with God who is love.

[36] Matt. 16:25.

Chapter 3

The Father as Christ

"This love is an eminently human one since it is directed from one person to another through an affection of the will; it involves the good of the whole person, and therefore can enrich the expressions of body and mind with a unique dignity, ennobling these expressions as special ingredients and signs of the friendship distinctive of marriage. This love God has judged worthy of special gifts, healing, perfecting, and exalting gifts of grace and of charity. Such love, merging the human with the divine, leads the spouses to a free and mutual gift of themselves, a gift providing itself by gentle affection and by deed; such love pervades the whole of their lives: indeed by its busy generosity it grows better and grows greater. Therefore it far excels mere erotic inclination, which, selfishly pursued, soon enough fades wretchedly away."

Pastoral Constitution on the
Church in the Modern World, no. 49

"Christian spouses, in virtue of the sacrament of Matrimony . . . signify and partake of the mystery of that unity and fruitful love which exists between Christ and His Church."

Dogmatic Constitution on the Church, no. 11

We tried in the last chapter to tell why love is not just a matter of the emotions and the senses. The extreme of looking upon the human person as merely an animal — which is the mistake of the sensualists — has its direct opposite in that error which denies the body and which used to be called angelism. Both extremes are the result of dualism, of thinking of the human person as a two-story building, the top floor being the "spiritual half" and the bottom floor being the "physical half." Some want to live in the upstairs and ignore the downstairs; more seem to live in the downstairs without realizing that there is an upstairs. Others would live in the elevator and spend their lives going up or down as the momentary occasion seems to warrant.

This whole notion is fostered and strengthened by those preachers and writers who, as much because of the limitations of language as for any reason, find it expedient to make clear and swift distinctions between a person's "higher" and "lower" natures, the "spiritual" and "animal" self, between a person's "lofty" or "base" motives, and so on.

With dualism, too sharp a dichotomy is made between the human body and soul; the soul, we are warned, should dominate the body, or else the "bestial part" of the person will rise up and tear him to pieces. Such warnings are not without some validity, but they tend to leave one with the impression that God gave us a beautiful second-story apartment to live in, but for some odd and unexplained reason put underneath it a downstairs full of dark, unhealthy, and menacing animals called "instincts," "drives," and "appetites," all of which are wicked and will devour us.

This is tragic, this thinking of oneself as a two-story building; it is tragic because it does not conform to reality. Having notions of things that do not conform to the reality of things as God made them is the hothouse of anxieties, neuroses, and mental illness. The unfortunate father who thinks of himself as a soul living on top of a body that is somehow unclean is likely to find life miserable. Marriage, since it is rooted in sex, will cause him the deepest mental distress, for he must express the highest feelings of his spirit in physical ways.

Human beings are a unity of body and soul

The Christian, however, should know that people are not two-story buildings; they do not have two natures, animal and spiritual, but one human nature. People are made up of matter and spirit, but we are not souls living on top of bodies; we are a body-soul unity. We can speak of the soul (including intelligence and free will) as "higher" than the body in the sense that it is the soul that is the image of God, but we should not conclude from this that the body is to be despised. Only a soul united with a body makes up a human person. The wound done to humankind by Original Sin was not done to the body alone, nor to the soul alone, but to our body-soul unity.

The disorder we personally experience in ourselves as the result of that wound is as often a matter of the soul (the will failing to respond to the intellect) as it is of the body (the senses thrusting aside the dictates of reason). The Christian knows, too, that even , as the Church upholds the immortality of the soul, she defends at every point the high dignity of the body. The Son of God became a human being with a fully human body that included sexuality. That same fully human body died and went through the incomprehensibly mysterious transformation that the Gospels refer to with the true but inadequate term *resurrection*. These facts alone should give pause to those who think of the human body as somehow ignoble, a small mistake God made when He created us.

Sex is a union of persons — not just bodies

The call to love another person within the sacrament of marriage is a call to love that person not only with the goodwill that we ought to show toward all, but also sexually. In marriage, a man is called to love a woman with his whole self, with his soul and his body. Marriage is the coming together neither of two souls nor of two bodies, but of two persons. Their union is really a "comm-union," a unique, deeply pleasurable oneness of body and soul, and this union of husband and wife was willed by God from the beginning.

But why, throughout all of nature, from the pistils and stamens of plants to the male and female of insects, birds, animals, and people, did God introduce sexuality? We know that an act of God accomplished this, but why?

Since the image of the Creator is in all that God has created, and since sexuality is one of the most vibrant chords resounding throughout creation, God must find in sexuality something beautiful and truly expressive of the divine nature. Can there be more meaning yet in married love?

In the Gospels, Jesus insists upon the inviolability of the marriage bond as the work of God. We know, too, that, guided by the Holy Spirit, the Church includes marriage as one of the seven sacraments, crowning the natural institution of marriage with a special holiness. Indeed, the letter to the Ephesians describes the union of husband and wife as a union in Christ.

Headship does not mean domination

In the words of Pope John Paul II: "When St. Paul wrote that 'wives should be submissive to their husbands as to the Lord,'[37] he did not mean that the husband is 'boss' of the wife and the interpersonal pact of matrimony is a pact of domination of husband over wife. There is to be no one-sided domination. Each is to be subject to the other from a sense of Christian piety."

A husband shows his love for his wife by being Christ-like in his self-sacrifice. The love of husband for wife is meant to be so unhesitatingly selfless that it will not stop short of the complete sacrifice of life itself for the good of the beloved, even as Christ died on the Cross for His Bride, the Church, which is us. Few, however, are asked actually to die for those they love; what is normally required of us is patience, generosity, and good humor, as well as an awareness of the needs of our wives and a willingness to meet those needs.

Marital intimacy must mirror the love of Christ

Material care is necessary, of course, but far less important to a woman than the knowledge that she is loved, wanted, and respected by her husband. Only in the security of the knowledge that she is loved can she give totally of herself. The husband who has allowed his love-demonstrations to become a matter of an occasional "romantic" moment, or has let his love-making become a bedroom routine, or has allowed the very thought of love-signs to wither away as the years have gone by, is asking for trouble

[37] Cf. Eph. 5:22.

in his marriage. Also, he has stunted his own growth as a man. His maturity was meant to come through his dedication to becoming a more skilled and sensitive lover in every dimension of his marriage.

Our land is full of men and women so unfulfilled: women unsure of being wanted; women starved for intimacy; women who feel their one task is to protect their spouse's ego, lest he become surly; women, who must constantly cater to men so unaware of themselves that they refuse to share responsibility for household tasks — even when their wives work full-time outside the home.

Even when the high fires of the wedding day are not quite reduced to the burnt charcoal of the divorce courtroom, the radiance can be allowed to die out. What was a mutual desire to give, an outward flow of the self to the other, has become only a desire to receive, a grasping after personal warmth that masquerades as love. The intimacy of marriage has become the source not of mutual enrichment, but of mutual impoverishment.

This need not be so; indeed, it is so only because men and women have permitted their love to become in a sense sacrilegious. They have reduced a sacred and holy relationship, a relationship which mirrors that of Christ with His Church, to the level of the profane. They have turned away from the life of God that flows through their marriage; they have denied the life of God in their spouses.

Husband and wife help each other get to Heaven

We should remind ourselves often that the woman we have married is beloved by God, indeed, that God dwells within her. We should remind ourselves that she has a life in God and that we have an obligation through our marriage vows to do what we can to nourish that life. We should remember to thank God for the gift of this woman, to ask God's blessing upon her, that we might be worthy of the calling He has given us. The "I love you" whispered to her should carry a benediction: "May you be richly blessed."

Holiness is the goal of marriage. By helping his wife to be the person God wants her to be, by encouraging in her the personality uniquely her own — the personality that he and perhaps only he among men knows and loves — a woman's husband helps her to grow in holiness. Was it not that vision of her uniqueness that overwhelmed him? Was this not what he "saw" that others did not see? The husband who allows no spiritual or psychological disfigurement to come about through his selfishness will find that his marriage will be a continuously richer experience as the years advance. As husband and wife grow closer to God, they are themselves more closely united; and the closer they grow to each other, the closer they grow to God.

One flesh with each other, in the Body of Christ

The letter to the Ephesians says "husbands should love their wives as their own bodies. He who loves his wife loves himself."[38] Earlier we caught a glimpse of what loving others as we love ourselves means; here, the Pauline tradition repeats Christ's command, but adds to it a particular emphasis: the married man is truly loving himself when he shows love to his wife, for she is bound to him not only by the spirit, but also by the strongest of all ties. "For no man ever hates his own flesh, but nourishes and cherishes it, as Christ does the Church, because we are members of His body."[39]

Through our baptism, we are incorporated into Christ, and through that union with Christ we participate in the very life of

---

[38] Eph. 5:28.
[39] Eph. 5:29-30.

God as it flows unceasingly from Christ to His Body, the Church. The early Church was full of the realization of the immensity, the almost unbearable greatness of the divine adoption. "See what love the Father has given us," calls out the first letter of John, "that we should be called the children of God."[40]

If we are children of the Father, it is because we "have put on Christ."[41] Like water mixed with wine, we have come, as the liturgy of the Eucharist says, "to share in the divinity of Christ, who humbled Himself to share in our humanity." All that we do is done "through Him, with Him, and in Him."

Christ is the principle of marital unity

This oneness of Christ with His Church is the reality that our marriages image. But we are limited creatures and cannot expect perfect unity in marriage. Personalities are not obliterated at the altar, and adjustments must be made by each spouse. The very differences between man and woman that attracted them to each other may become the source of difficulties after the wedding day, but in seeking unity with each other, they shall find happiness, pleasure, joy, and the wholeness of a mature marriage.

Ill will arises when either spouse seeks not unity, but something for the self that is counter to the good of the marriage, the gratification of some personal desire that will not also nourish the marriage. Ill will is destructive of unity; it is the root of isolation. The husband who bears ill will cannot claim to love, for to love is to will good. And the man who does not love is a man isolated, a man who will never find unity, for in order to know those fleeting moments of rapture that dazzle the consciousness with their beauty,

---

[40] 1 John 3:1.
[41] Gal. 3:27.

there must be a surrender of the self, a full giving in love. For union with God happens only through love.

But if a man should not bear ill will to his own flesh and blood, it is not solely because they are his flesh and blood, but because they are Christ's. The caresses husband and wife exchange are caresses given to Christ, as well. The body touched with the fingertips belongs to Christ, is given in Christ. And the fingers that touch are meant to be Christ's, too, and the love they express is meant to be a love that increases the married couple's intimacy with each other and with Christ.

The more perfectly the husband identifies his place in the family with that of Christ and the more he strives to pattern himself and his giving after Christ, the more perfectly will his marriage image the union of Christ and His people, the Church. " 'For this reason a man shall leave his father and his mother and be joined to his wife, and the two shall become one.' This is a great mystery, and I mean in reference to Christ and the Church."[42]

Marriage: earthly symbol of the
union between Christ and His Church

Is there any mystery more difficult to penetrate than that of the union of Christ and ourselves, His Church, a real supernatural union of Christ and each individual Christian that binds all into a oneness? For Paul, it was the mystery of the Gospel; all else flows from it. And here, Paul tells us explicitly that this mystery is intimately related to the mystery of marriage.

By quoting Hebrew Scriptures, Paul reminds us that marriage was divinely ordained from the beginning; in applying those words to Christ and His Church, he unveils for us that the marriage

---

[42] Eph. 5:31-32.

union between a Christian man and a Christian woman is a symbolizing of — a making real in a mysterious way — the union of Christ and His people. As there is but one Bride, the Church, and one Bridegroom, Christ, so the marriage bond unites one man and one woman. They have a total commitment until death.

Jesus underscored not only this unity, but also its indissolubility when He said that "what therefore God has joined together, let no man put asunder."[43] Just as God has joined Himself permanently to His people in Christ, so, too, does a sacramental marriage join husband and wife in a permanent union that human beings cannot dissolve.

Marriage is a vessel for grace

Moreover, the union of Christ and His people, the Church, has as its purpose the union of human beings with God's self-gift (grace). The marriage union has as its purpose the birth of human persons into this natural life so that they may enter into an eternal union with Christ that begins on this earth. The "seed" of the husband flowing into the womb of the wife to spark new life was seen by the early Greek Fathers of the Church as a symbol of the self-gift, or grace, of Christ flowing into His Bride, the Church, to generate saints.

This symbolizing is the living out of the holiness specific to marriage. In the marital union, to make love is the outward sign that, working with God, communicates intimacy with God to each other; it is an encounter with the risen Christ, who is present and active in a special way during this pleasure-filled union; it is a living realization of the life-giving union of Christ with the Church.

[43] Matt. 19:6.

The first gift of husband and wife to each other is God's self-gift, the gift of abundant life, which Christ brought to us. "I came so that they may have life and have it abundantly."[44] Throughout their married life, in all their attempts to help each other to be happy, when they rejoice in shared sexual pleasure and in all their shared experiences, joyous and heartbreaking, spouses will continue to be for each other the instruments of divine life.

Every grace received by husband or wife, including God's self-gift carried by the other sacraments, will be a grace to perfect them further and to help them fulfill their high and difficult vocation of faithfully imaging the union of the risen Christ with the Church.

Fathers must imitate the love and authority of God

The vocation of husband also becomes the vocation of father when the married people become parents, either by giving birth or through adoption. It is not surprising that the letter to the Ephesians, immediately after discussing the relationship between husband and wife, turns to a consideration of the relationship of parent and child. "Children, obey your parents in the Lord, for this is right. 'Honor your father and mother (this is the first commandment with a promise) that it may be well with you and that you may live long on the earth.' "[45]

Still, none of us should invoke the commandment without pondering the words that follow and complete it: "Fathers, do not provoke your children to anger, but bring them up in the discipline and instruction of the Lord."[46]

[44] John 10:10.
[45] Eph. 6:1-3.
[46] Eph. 6:4.

"Of the Lord." "In the Lord." All members of a family are equal before God; all are unique and sacred personalities destined for the same eternal life. The natural hierarchy of authority in the family is protected from abuse by those words, "of the Lord."

It is not for himself that the father serves his family, but as a minister of Christ. Not only can he not require anything from his children contrary to Christian principles, but also he must see to it that children subject to the authority shared by him and his wife are formed in Christ, through a discipline rooted in love and aimed at the gradual independence of the children as they mature.

The Christian father teaches and trains

Surely the father who makes the consequences of a child's unacceptable act inappropriate to the act fails to discipline as the Lord would do. Remember that "to discipline" means "to teach." The tyrannical parent, the selfish or unfair parent — and how quickly children recognize unfairness! — is the one who rouses his child to constant, deep-seated resentment and rebellion. Such fathers are, however, probably just as common as those who are overindulgent or indifferent, who refuse to discipline their children at all.

This lack of correction often disguises itself as love. These fathers rouse their children to resentment, too, the resentment the child feels at not having the order and serenity that only authority can impose and that the child subconsciously craves. In addition, parents who are tyrannical, overindulgent, or indifferent incite in the child a resentment of any later attempt to impose discipline or authority.

Does it sound strange that we should be told that it is the kind father who is quick to discipline, that the man who exercises his authority is the friend to his child? Yet any gardener knows that a beautiful flower or a healthy hedge is the result of pruning dead or wayward shoots. The undisciplined shrub, the unpruned rosebush, both soon turn ugly.

The father who loves his children — who wills their good — will not let them grow up without direction, training, and discipline. To do otherwise is to deprive them of that promise attached to their observance of the Fourth Commandment: "That it may be well with you and that you may live long on the earth." Nearly all of our "problem children," our wayward youth, all of those children with whom things have not gone well and who are not headed for "a long life on earth," come from homes where there was not a good, balanced sense of discipline and order.

The modern world presents special challenges

Christianity's revolutionary truth about marriage has been under attack in recent centuries. The rupture of Christendom, along with the secularization of society that rapidly followed, has dragged many back to a life lived by pagan standards.

Divorce, virtually unknown in the early ages of Christianity, is now a possibility for all. The pagan practices of polygamy and polyandry are with us in full force, with only slight alteration — spouses are now successive instead of simultaneous. Abortion, differing from the pagan practice of infanticide only by the fact that it occurs earlier (before birth), is legal and on the increase globally.

In addition, popular culture both trivializes and makes a god of sex. In one sense, the ancient pagan cults had more balance, for they at least reverenced sex as a mystery. Today's entertainment and advertising media see sex only as a sort of toy. Ironically enough, this return to a world of pseudo-paganism, this rejection of the new and return to the old, is thought by a huge number of people to be "progress."

One of the more important factors behind this return to false paganism has been the decline of the sense of the sacred among humankind, the loss of that awareness of God's reflection in all of creation. The popular deification of science, most common among nonscientists, has stunted in the souls of many the sense of mystery, of awe and reverence before the wonders of God. "Be subordinate to one another," the letter to the Ephesians instructs spouses, "out of reverence for Christ."[47] But if "reverence for Christ" diminishes?

Secular society is at odds with Christian marriage

Basically, the disintegration of the family has kept pace with the loss of Christ-consciousness. With the secularization of society that followed the Protestant Reformation in the sixteenth century, people have had the consciousness of their oneness with Christ washed from their minds. When the Church split and, in effect began to battle with herself, the sense of the Church as a reliable guide crumbled for society at large. But Christ is wed to His people, the Church, and it was inevitable that with the loss of Church-consciousness, people should lose their consciousness of Christ.

The effect of this on the family was immediate, for it is only in full awareness of their union with God that people can adequately fulfill their roles as spouses and parents. If fathers and mothers can no longer look upon themselves as called to a holy project, as called to bring God's love into the home, how can they possibly look upon their relationship with each other as one with their relationship with Christ? And if they do not see this, what basis is there for husband and wife to be submissive to each other in Christ?

---

[47] Cf. Eph. 5:21.

The husband who understands that what goes on in marriage is nothing more or less than what goes on between Christ and the Church can see the pattern he is to follow, can understand the meaning of unity, indissolubility, love, fruitfulness, and holiness as they exist in marriage. But what about the man who is insensible to Christ? Couples having the highest ideals but lacking the life that flows through the marriage that is a sacrament cannot be more to each other than each one is. What if the marriage ever demands more than this? Who can guarantee himself that it never will?

Is it to avoid crises too severe for their unaided love that such couples sometimes avoid having children? And what about couples who do not have the highest ideals? The unity they think they have found in the pleasure of sex may endure for a while, but the sum of human experience tells us that this is a false unity and that all attempts to found unity on sexual desire alone are doomed. Desire is not love, but an invitation to love. A marriage not based on love is destined to fail.

A new kind of paganism threatens the family

The return to paganism that we see as a result of the loss of Christ-consciousness is not a return to the paganism of the pre-Christian West, however much appearances may seem to proclaim it. A society devoid of God-consciousness is of necessity inferior to the pagan civilization that preceded it. One reason for this is that all the good in paganism was "baptized," caught up, and brought into the service of Christ. Thus, even the nominally Christian home today that has not the headship of Christ lacks all headship whatsoever.

Christians are not alone in deploring the disintegration of family life that has followed the flood of neopaganism. Researchers and writers of goodwill with no religious perspective have for years been seeking ways to restore life to those unhappy homes that are the chief victims of moral erosion and that are now the source of so many of our social ills. Valiant as some of these endeavors might be, most, if not all, of them are doomed to failure because they treat only the symptoms and do not attack the social diseases themselves.

Some do hint at the spiritual roots of the illness when they urge families to attend church together, but more often than not this advice stems from the erroneous notion that religion is meant to serve humankind rather than to be our way of worshiping God. To recommend religion as one might prescribe a pill is to make banal the highest activity of the human heart. God is "the first and the last, the beginning and the end."[48] To treat God as a psychological or social prop is to mock Him.

Modern solutions account for changing roles

Many popular writers, however, offer solutions to the problems posed by family disintegration from which God is altogether excluded. Some talk of the family as a "team" to be ruled entirely by democratic procedure and see a stronger home life issuing from a voting arrangement whereby all members of the family will have a voice in important family decisions.

Democratic procedure, if it is not to be carried to absurd extremes, must be controlled and have its limits when one is dealing with children. Even if parents were willing — and there seems to be no mass movement toward this sort of thing — there are numerous decisions that children are totally unqualified to make and that parents must make for them.

[48] Rev. 22:13.

Head of the Family

Actually, the partnership idea of shared headship in the family is the dominant notion today. Modern living has done away with many old distinctions between masculine and feminine roles, in the workplace and in the home. Our grandfathers would no more have thought of changing the baby's diapers than our grandmothers would have considered building a barn. There is a much greater collaboration today between husband and wife in business, social, and political affairs than at any time in the past. This increased intimacy has its value in that it binds husband and wife closer together in their mutual task.

When both husband and wife work outside the home, however, this raises issues that many people struggle with today. Who will be responsible for child care? Who will clean the house and prepare the meals? In many cases at the present time, wives and mothers find themselves with two full-time jobs: one in the workplace, another at home. No husband and father with any sense of justice and fair play will fail to strive in such a situation to attain a better balance. This will require his willingness to shoulder his share of responsibilities in the home and with the children. No such husband and father will forget that his family needs his presence at least as much as the money he earns.

Shared time — time husband and wife spend away from the children nurturing their relationship — is important to the family. Time span in interaction with the children — whether in play or helping with homework — helps to keep open the channels of communication between parent and child.

The Christian father — by his style of being what he is called to be — opens for His children a pathway through the jungle of contemporary civilization and its scary swamps. By working toward an ever-deepening love relationship with their mother, he lets them know what a healthy marriage is. By devoting time and attention

54

to them, he affirms their feelings of security not only in his love, but in God's love.

Popular culture can poison the Christian family

There are many television programs and movies where the father is the butt of jokes or where he seems effortlessly to provide his family with a fantastically high standard of living. Meanwhile, the National Education Association reported that ninety-two percent of all sexual encounters on television take place between unmarried people. When was the last time we saw a passionate love embrace between husband and wife? It doesn't happen on television — although we do see one murder an hour. By the time he is eighteen years old, the average child will have spent twice as many hours before a television set than in a classroom.

If the notion of the family is an impoverished one, emptied of meaning for many, that is but a testimonial to the degree of damage already done by the secular atmosphere in which we live. The best antidote to such a poisonous atmosphere is the creation of a Christian home.

The next time we see "father" being made the boob of the story, it might be worthwhile for us to compare the role of this "father" with the high dignity and rich meaning of Christian fatherhood. Renewal can come, for fathers and their families, through Christ, who says, "Behold, I make all things new."[49]

Let marriage become all that it is

When we fathers become aware of "His precious and very great promises"[50] given to us, that we are sharers in the divine nature;

---

[49] Rev. 21:5.
[50] 2 Pet. 1:4.

when we see that our marriage is meant to reflect the marriage between Christ and His Bride, the Church, which is the archetype
and foundation of all truly Christian marriages — then will the
water of our marriages be, as at Cana, changed to wine by the love
of Christ. Then we will have set our feet on the path that leads to
"the marriage of the Lamb."[51]

---

[51] Rev. 19:7.

Chapter 4

The Father as Priest

"The training for the apostolate should start with the children's earliest education. In a special way, however, adolescents and young persons should be initiated into the apostolate and imbued with its spirit. This formation must be perfected throughout their whole life in keeping with the demands of new responsibilities. It is evident, therefore, that those who have the obligation to provide a Christian education also have the duty of providing formation for the apostolate. In the family parents have the task of training their children from childhood on to recognize God's love for all men. By example especially they should teach them little by little to be solicitous for the material and spiritual needs of their neighbor. The whole family in its common life, then, should be a sort of apprenticeship for the apostolate. Children must be educated, too, in such fashion that, transcending the family circle, they may open their minds to both ecclesiastical and temporal communities. They should be so involved in the local community of the parish that they will acquire a conscious-ness of being living and active members of the people of God."

Decree on the Apostolate of the Laity, no. 30

In the late fourth century A.D., St. John Chrysostom,[52] one of the early Fathers of the Church, called the Christian family *ekklesia,* which is the Greek New Testament term for "Church." The truth that the family is a "domestic Church" is worth reflection.

There are today countries in the world where the Church is kept alive only in the home, where — with priests imprisoned or executed and any public manifestation of religion forbidden — the only accessible sacraments are Baptism and marriage. The entire religious life of the family must be carried on in the hidden recesses of the home. In such a situation the father of the family must know the profound responsibility and the true dignity, the priestly dignity, of his fatherhood.

We citizens of the United States lack the grace of such hardship — and such hardship is a grace if it leads us to better grasp how close God is to us. It is easier for us to lose sight of the responsibilities that the father shares in common with a priest: manifold responsibilities as teacher, counselor, spiritual director, and leader in liturgical prayer. If we may call an ordained priest "Father" and by that refer to his true if not actual paternal relationship to the

---

[52] St. John Chrysostom (c. 347-407), Archbishop of Constantinople and Doctor; named Chrysostom, or "Golden Mouth" for his eloquent preaching.

community of believers, we may call the father "priest" and by that refer to his role as a guide in faith and as head of that domestic Church which is his family.

All believers participate in Christ's priesthood

Through the sacrament of Baptism, all Christians share in the priesthood of Christ, the High Priest. "You were made a priest at Baptism," St. John Chrysostom says. His words were echoed many years ago by Pope Pius XII, who said that while the priest alone has the power to consecrate the bread and wine, it is by virtue of their lay priesthood that laypersons can join with the priest in celebrating the Eucharist.

"Nor is it to be wondered at," Pius XII wrote, "that the faithful should be raised to this dignity. By the waters of Baptism, as by common right, Christians are made members of the Mystical Body of Christ the Priest, and by the 'character' which is imprinted on their souls, they are appointed to give worship to God. Thus, they participate, according to their condition, in the priesthood of Christ."

It is by and through their incorporation in the Body of Christ, their sharing in His priesthood, that two Christians are able to confer upon each other the sacrament of Matrimony. It is wrong to say of some couple that "Father So-and-so married them," for he did not. They married each other; they were the ministers of the sacrament. Father So-and-so was but the Church's witness at that moment they conferred upon each other that sacrament which would unite them in a lifelong union that is an image of Christ's loving union with His Church.

This is not to put the sacrament of marriage outside the Church. By no means! As the theologian Karl Rahner put it, the married couple constitutes the smallest genuine form of the Church.

A Christian life is a life in which the Eucharist plays a central role, for the life of the Christian is constantly refreshed and strengthened by this basic act of Christian worship. The Mass is a communal act of worship, a social act rather than a time for private devotions, and the family, as a microcosm of the Church, should, if at all possible, participate in it together.

A father and mother attending Mass with their children to offer thanks to God, and to renew their loving intimacy with Christ and with one another, participate in an action that is essential to their life together.

Help your kids to love the Mass

Children can sometimes create a distraction at Mass, but this can be countered by a little advance preparation and common sense. First, the children should be imbued with a spirit of reverence for the Mass before they are brought to church. This is not something one does with a threat before entering the church, but through fostering an attitude in all their prayer times and by the whole atmosphere at home. Children who realize that attendance at Mass is a high point in the life of their family, although they may still give their parents some difficult moments, eventually will come to understand the need for proper behavior in church.

Parents should not be above establishing a logical consequence or two when it comes to children's behavior during Mass. Some parents tie behavior at Mass to a reward system: excellent behavior rates a frosted doughnut. So-so behavior merits a plain cake doughnut. And unacceptable behavior means no doughnut at all. In order for this to work, however, parents must not go back on their part of the agreement.

Another praiseworthy approach to dealing with children in church is to be sure that when they are little, parents give them plenty of hugs, plenty of holding and caressing in church. Babies and toddlers who associate lots of physical affection with being in church are likely to be less of a problem later on.

Even young children often find the Mass fascinating, especially if their parents are wise enough to sit in a front pew where children can see what's going on. For the Mass is a drama, a liturgical drama clothed in colorful vestments, often surrounded by floral displays and candles. Even a child too young to understand much of what is taking place can find something to interest him.

The father should simply call the wandering attention of his children back to the ritual by pointing out what is going on. The distracting child at Mass is the bored child, the child frightened by a sea of strange heads, or the child deserted in the midst of a strange group of people while one or the other of his parents is going to receive Holy Communion.

Parents should bring their children with them when they go to receive Communion, and today some priests and ministers of the Eucharist give the child a blessing at that time, which helps the child to feel more included.

Some might have reservations about teaching children during Mass. Yet there is no reason why the father or mother should not whisper brief explanations to the children at various points during the Mass. In this, parents fulfill one of the obligations of the priest-hood of the laity: the religious instruction of their children.

Reverence in Church begins at home

The whole atmosphere at home is important to fostering in the children a proper attitude toward the Eucharist. This should not be an isolated hour of worship in an otherwise secular week — but this is exactly what it will be to our children if that is what it is to us.

If God is the supreme reality and the highest good in our lives, then this will make itself evident in our lives. The father who participates in the Mass regularly gives to his children a far more convincing statement as to the importance of the Mass than all his words do.

"One of the greatest things my father ever did for me," a friend once said, "was to take me aside one evening and tell me that I was old enough to go to Mass with him every morning if I wished. 'If I wished.' I wished nothing more. I'll never forget those silent walks to church in the quiet hours of the morning and our kneeling together at the Communion rail."

But if the principal act of Catholic worship is outside the home, within the home the Liturgy has a place, too. No father should be ignorant of the many valuable pamphlets and books on family prayer and rituals. The responsibility of a father is first and foremost to provide an environment that will enable his children to advance in wisdom and age and favor before God and humankind.[53]

Such a home environment is not produced merely by purchasing religious objects for the walls or by playing lots of Christian music on the stereo; rather, it is produced by the tone of the life that is lived there.

The father bears witness by how he lives

As North Americans, we seem to have a natural impulse to look for a technique that will give us the desired results in any particular field. We always want to know what we must do in order to accomplish our ends. In certain areas — building a house, flying an airplane, operating a computer — the matter of technical knowledge, knowing what to do and when to do it, is crucial. But

[53] Cf. Luke 2:52.

we must not allow our talent for technique to lead us astray when we approach the realm of the spirit.

In the religious sphere it is not so much *doing* that counts, as it is *being*. To do an act of charity without being charitable — giving money to a beggar to get rid of him or to let others see how charitable we are — is not to do an act of charity at all. In fact, such an act can be a sin of selfishness or pride. To adorn the home with crucifixes or pictures of the saints is meaningless — and can be a travesty — unless these things are an expression of the life that is lived there. And that life must be a life lived in Christ.

The Eucharist never ends. As the Second Vatican Council, in the mid-1960s, pointed out in its *Dogmatic Constitution on the Church*, no. 10: "Christ the Lord, high priest taken from among men[54] made the new people 'a kingdom of priests to God, His Father.'[55] The baptized, by regeneration and the anointing of the Holy Spirit, are consecrated to be a spiritual house and a holy priesthood, that through all the works of Christian men they may offer spiritual sacrifices and proclaim the perfection of Him who has called them out of darkness into His marvelous light.[56] Therefore all the disciples of Christ, persevering in prayer and praising God,[57] should present themselves as a sacrifice, living, holy, and pleasing to God.[58] They should everywhere on earth bear witness to Christ and give an answer to everyone who asks a reason for the hope of an eternal life which is theirs."[59]

[54] Cf. Heb. 5:1-5.
[55] Rev. 1:6; cf. 5:9-10.
[56] Cf. 1 Pet. 2:4-10.
[57] Cf. Acts 2:42-47.
[58] Cf. Rom. 12:1.
[59] Cf. 1 Pet. 3:15.

The father of a family "bears witness" in a number of ways. Some we have already discussed; some will be mentioned in later chapters.

Here we might fruitfully pause to consider the fact that, in discussing the priesthood of all the faithful, the Second Vatican Council's *Dogmatic Constitution on the Church* took note of the fact that "In virtue of the Sacrament of Matrimony by which they signify and share[60] the mystery of the utility and faithful love between Christ and the Church, Christian married couples help one another to attain holiness in their married life and in the rearing of their children. Hence by reason of their state in life and of their position they have their own gifts in the People of God.[61] From the marriage of Christians there comes the family in which new citizens of human society are born, and, by the grace of the Holy Spirit received in Baptism, these are made children of God so that the People of God may be perpetuated throughout the centuries. In what might be regarded as the domestic Church, the parents, by word and example, are the first heralds of the Faith with regard to their children."[62]

So the natural parental role of educator of our children becomes, for the Christian father, a specific work of his lay priesthood: he is a "preacher of the Faith" to his children.

The father creates a Christian community in the home

A father has need to remember that the best testimony he can give to the Gospel is not in words but in deeds, in the quality of life that he creates in his "domestic Church." To aid him in making

[60] Cf. Eph. 5:32.
[61] Cf. 1 Cor. 7:7.
[62] No. 11.

his community one that is truly a Christian one, a joyful and loving one, the father of the family must do what he can to foster a spirit of prayer, celebration, thanksgiving — in short, a spirit of supernatural love in his community.

A father will find help in this task by fostering such Christian activities as family meal prayers (that are not merely a rote duty, but a time of familiar sharing) and by creating other times for family prayer and family rituals. The building up of family customs and traditions can become a part of the texture of the life of the worshiping community that the family is meant to be.

In recent years, we have seen many books and pamphlets published about family prayer and ritual. These have not only fostered but are also a sign of the increasing interest in Christian family life. Catholics have a rich treasury of rituals and traditions to help the family to grow in grace and be transformed in Christ. Which of these will most suit the needs of any specific family is best left up to the individual parents; but the minimum, it would seem, would be a return to the venerable custom of beginning the daily family meal with prayer.

The father who is fully conscious of the sacred duty that goes with the dignity of his fatherhood will, of course, with his wife seek further means to bring Christian truths alive in the minds and hearts of his children. Special days will be remembered in special ways: for example, the baptismal day of each child may be celebrated and his baptismal candle lighted for a few minutes at the principal meal while the father or mother reads again the baptismal promises.

As God's representatives in the home, parents are head of what has been called "the first and most important liturgical community." It is they who must guide their family through the liturgical year in ways appropriate to family life. Parents explain to their children the significance of each season and prepare them, each according to his or her understanding, for the great feasts.

The life of the home must be a liturgical life, a life lived in accord with the rhythms of the Church year. Christ's birth should be celebrated as Christ's birth and not as the time when a secular Santa Claus bestows largesse. To place a great deal of emphasis at Christmas on the department-store Santa Claus and to do the same at Easter with bunnies and chicks is not only to secularize these great feasts of the Church, but to endanger the faith of one's children. For when the child's belief in such things is shattered, it may be discovered that his faith in the reality of Easter and Christmas has been impaired. At the very least, his confidence in parents may be wounded. This consideration alone should give us pause, but there is the larger consideration of our duty to Christ that cannot be ignored if we wish even to begin to live as Christians.

The paternal blessing is a beautiful expression of our priestly role

Practically all the religious practices concerned with the home require parental leadership, whether it be the leading of family prayers, the saying of grace, or the blessing of the Advent wreath. The father is the spiritual leader of this sacred community. To refuse on such occasions to exercise his lay priesthood, this spiritual leadership, cripples the family's religious life. When the father does not exercise his spiritual leadership, for example, it can make the boys of the family susceptible to the argument that "religion is for women." While we must save details of specific religious customs and rituals for the home — leaving these considerations now to the discernment of the father and mother, who will find abundant material available on the subject — there is one practice that is so simple that no family could find it difficult to use, so beautiful that it demands our attention, and so full of meaning that a discussion of the priestly role of the father would not be complete without it. The tradition is that of the paternal blessing.

In our home, when our children were growing up, the parental blessing was given by having the children, in order of age, come to the holy water font after their evening prayers. There each child received the Sign of the Cross on his or her forehead with holy-water while the following words were spoken: "I bless you, [Name], my child, in the name of the Father and of the Son and of the Holy Spirit. Amen." Then followed a brief prayer to the child's patron saint.

Today, many parents use a simpler, less formal parental blessing. As he tucks his children into bed for the night, one father simply traces the Sign of the Cross on each child's forehead and says, "God be with you all through the night."

Actually, the father may use whatever words he thinks suitable for the occasion, even as the blessing itself need not be restricted to bedtimes. A child about to undergo surgery, to attend summer camp, to begin school, to graduate, or to be married, could receive the parental blessing. Nor need the practice be discontinued as the child progresses in years. Bishops have been known to kneel for their mother's blessing. That "man for all seasons," St. Thomas More, when lord chancellor of England, knelt for his father's blessing each morning.

What a mark of the father's dignity! What an exercise of his lay priesthood! What man would not be humbled by his recognition of the profound responsibility of such a power, the power of blessing his children? What man could bless his children and not himself feel blessed at having children? And what child could receive his father's blessing and not recognize that they are tied by a bond stronger than the flesh — that the father is here as God's representative?

The father, seeing himself as a channel of grace, is made more aware of his own reliance upon the grace of God, of his own responsibilities before God. The child who goes to bed with the touch of the father's hands upon his head and words of the father's blessing still fresh in his ears is a child secure in the knowledge of the love not only of an earthly father, but of the Father in Heaven.

Fathers shouldn't pass off these duties to others

Many Catholic fathers, however, seem to be unwilling to lead the spiritual life of their families, often abdicating spiritual authority to their wives instead of sharing it with them, as they should. These prefer to make the Eucharist an individualistic act of worship rather than a familial one, and as for prayer and ritual in the home, they don't want to be "different." They prefer to be *indifferent*.

Such fathers may assume that by having their children in a Catholic school or parish religious-education program, they have fulfilled their obligation as far as their spiritual guidance is concerned. They are wrong. A formal religious-education program, in a school or a parish, is a training in facts, a training based upon the assumption that at home those facts are placed by the parents into the context of everyday life.

No amount of formal learning about the Mass will be meaningful if the parents have not awakened a real spirit of sacrifice and thanksgiving in their children. And how do we explain the Mass as a "corporate act of worship" if that most basic corporate unit, family, does not worship together?

St. Paul speaks of our making up what is lacking in the sufferings of Christ. A startling statement, but it tells us that we must carry Christ to others, must help to apply the merits of His sacrifice to the world. We must do this, lest we be forced to apply to ourselves those words in the Gospel of John: "He was in the world, and the world was made though Him, yet the world knew Him not. He came to His own home, and His own people received Him not."[63]

There are homes, too many homes, where Christ has no welcome, where the liturgical year is known only vaguely as something that happens "in church." The great feasts pass by with only a nod, the family is embarrassed to pray together, and Christ is a stranger in the conversations and plans of the family. These are homes where the father (and mother) of the family have either never recognized their lay priesthood or never chosen to exercise it. These are homes without spiritual leadership.

Parenthood is holy work

God dwells in our children. When we confront this reality, when we grasp this notion and what it means, we cannot but sense the sacredness of our paternal vocation. God has not only granted to us the unspeakable privilege of sharing with Him in creation, by allowing us to help in the formation of human persons; He has also given us the sacred trust of raising up these persons as fit dwelling-places for His own presence on earth and sharers in His eternal life.

This is the holy work that we, as parents, are called upon to perform, and this is, at root, the reason our homes constitute the most basic unit of the Church — why they are, indeed, sacred places. This, too, is the reason St. Augustine[64] called the fathers of

---

[63] John 1:10-11.

[64] St. Augustine (354-430), Bishop of Hippo.

families "My fellow bishops." What a glorious title is ours if we bring Christ into our homes, the Gospel of John tells us: "But to all who received Him, who believed in His name, He gave power to become children of God; who are born, not of blood nor of the will of the flesh nor of the will of man, but of God."[65]

[65] John 1:12-13.

Chapter 5

The Father as Teacher

"Since parents have given children their life, they are bound by the most serious obligation to educate their offspring and therefore must be recognized as the primary and principal educators. This role in education is so important that only with difficulty can it be supplied where it is lacking. Parents are the ones who must create a family atmosphere animated by love and respect for God and man, in which the well-rounded personal and social education of children is fostered. Hence the family is the first school of the social virtues that every society needs. It is particularly in the Christian family, enriched by the grace and office of the sacrament of Matrimony, that children should be taught from their early years to have a knowledge of God according to the faith received in Baptism, to worship Him, and to love their neighbor. Here, too, they find their first experience of a wholesome human society and of the Church. Finally, it is through the family that they are gradually led to a companionship with their fellowmen and with the people of God. Let parents, then, recognize the inestimable importance a truly Christian family has for the life and progress of God's own people."

Declaration on Christian Education, no. 3

We all need heroes, especially when we are children: people we honor for outstanding qualities and whose accomplishments give us some guide whereby to judge our own success or failure.

For the Christian there is, ultimately, but one hero, one person worthy of emulation: Jesus Christ, Son of God and Son of man. For the Christian all true heroism is rooted in the imitation of Christ and all true heroes are saints, those Christians who most effectively made their lives an imitation of His.

But for the child, his first heroes will be his parents. Thus, even a very young child will put on Dad's hat or Mom's shoes and try to imitate parental behavior. Few parents are unfamiliar with some revealing episode in the play of their children when one child has assumed the role of the father or mother and mouthed the parent's exact words! More universal even than this is the commonplace occurrence of the child at table desirous of a fork because "Daddy has a fork," or a "glass like Mommy's."

The father's place as hero in the lives of his children is one that rests upon his positive and clear role in the home. If he has shrugged off active involvement as a leader in the home, if he consigns this to the limbo to which he consigns all that he is "too busy" to do, or has allowed his business interests to cut him off from his family, then his children will seek a hero elsewhere.

Fathers must compete with false heroes

Children do this because they need authority, they need a guide; and that authority and that guide must be a person. Children, especially the very young, do not reach rational conclusions and then set their wills upon the accomplishment of ends they deem good. The Church has traditionally maintained that a child does not reach the age of reason and the exercise of free will until approximately his seventh year.

Before that time, and even after it for many children, their apprehension of the good and the bad in human life (which translates into their ideals and their actions) is based upon the very concrete data offered by those around them. They look about for a norm, for somebody to follow, and if they do not find that norm in their parents, they will surely find it in one of the many pseudo-heroes on TV or from among sports or rock-music superstars.

Years ago, the newspapers carried the report of a man who had accidentally wounded his infant son while practicing a "fast draw" with a pistol. The investigation that followed led to the discovery that his front room was full of bullet holes from previous attempts to outdraw the villain of a TV western. Gradually it came to light that this man was not alone, but that he had his counterparts all across the country, men who were doing their best to imitate the mythic heroes of the TV western.

While psychiatric examination in particular cases might reveal other factors, I think one could safely generalize that these men suffered from a malady peculiar to a "post-Christian" world: lacking true heroes to worship, they chose to emulate the activities of artificial ones. If grown men took these false heroes for true, how much more readily will an unsophisticated child do the same.

That the father has to compete with pseudo-heroes on TV and in professional sports — whose jobs are easy because they last only as long as the program or televised game, while the father's heroism must be consistently observable in his every contact with his family — is a real hazard and has struck a blow at the emulation of the father as hero. Yet, it is a hazard that can and must be met.

To form children, we must let Christ form us

The solution lies not only in a much more judicious use of the TV set, but in reforming our own lives under the influence of the Gospel and the Spirit of Christ. It is not any artificial pose we are called upon to assume — children, lacking guile themselves, are quick to spot deceit in others — but a true union of ourselves with Christ.

Some modern psychologists contend that the psychic states of the parents at the time of conception have a tremendous influence upon the personality of the child; some go so far as to claim that the basic personality of the child is formed by the time he is three years old. Without accepting these claims — indeed, rejecting outright those based on denial of free will and the workings of divine grace — we can yet see the truth underlying them: the first months and years of a child's life exert immeasurable influence over the future development of the human person.

Pope Pius XII said to parents many years ago concerning their offspring, "It is your task from the cradle to begin their education in soul as well as in body; for if you do not educate them, they will begin, for good or ill, to educate themselves." How many children in the United States are thrown back upon their own resources, are educating themselves because they are not being educated by their parents? Scanning of the morning newspaper provides unscientific but sufficient evidence that the education of too many has been self-education and, for that reason, an education in selfishness.

It is in the molding of the wax of young lives that the fathers of families enjoy one of their highest privileges. Even as they are co-creators with God of this human person, so they are cooperators with God in the high artistry that strives to form Christ in the child.

The artist is called *homo faber:* man the maker. What more prodigious making is there than that which collaborates with God in the making of a human being! As St. John Chrysostom wrote: "What greater work is there than training the young mind and forming the habits of the young?" And this work is first and foremost the work of fathers and mothers.

Indeed, parents have far more power to influence their children than many are aware of today, assuming that they do not abdicate this power to television, movies, and a school system that insists that the existence of God is merely a matter of private personal opinion, a subject of indifference in the classroom.

If fathers don't model manhood, the culture will

The infantilism of the hero-worship displayed by the man mentioned earlier in this chapter reflects more upon his father than upon himself. His father apparently never filled the need in his son's life for a hero on the human level, nor pointed out to him that there were more important indications of a man's strength and integrity than how quickly one could mow down a bunch of bad guys with a gun. A whole generation is growing up between the old "macho" criteria of manhood and the more recent — admittedly legitimate — concern that men be sensitive and caring. What is a man, anyway? Is a man merely a guy who is good with a baseball bat or a basketball and knows how to repair a car?

The truth is that boys are being molded by hands other than those of their fathers; the minds and hearts of the young are being formed by advertisers and money-seekers without consciences.

Kenneth L. Woodward, a senior writer for *Newsweek* magazine and a Catholic, says: "In this society . . . I see the young captured by a vapid, boring, commercialized youth culture and not interested in becoming adults. Someone has got to show them that adulthood requires character and commitment."

Children are looked upon by those who manipulate them through television, magazines, and movies as a "market" and the moment the market for the latest status-symbol toy is overstocked, another one takes over.

"See that you do not despise any of these little ones," Jesus cautions us in Matthew's Gospel, "for I tell you that in Heaven their angels always behold the face of my Father who is in Heaven."[66] This warning should take root in the hearts of parents, particularly of fathers, for in neglecting their young, casting their children upon outside forces, and letting them be molded willy-nilly by circumstances and the mass media, they cannot escape the fact that they are "despising" their children.

Make the home a haven

The home was once a haven from the outside world. In it, in its quiet and closeted atmosphere, the work of educating the young could go on apace with relatively little competition. When we welcomed radio and especially television into the home, however, for better and for worse, all of the outside world flowed into the intimacy of the family environment.

Where the father of a family once may have read from the *Lives of the Saints* or the Bible in the evening, an anonymous voice now reads or sings from a script that extols the virtues of soft drinks, contraceptives, beer, refrigerators, automobiles, or tampons. One

---

[66] Matt. 18:10.

author, Marie Winn, wrote a best-selling book about the impact of television on family life and titled it *The Plug-in Drug*.

Where before a child could be protected and made aware gradually and in keeping with his age level of the evil and less desirable aspects of life in the world at large, and of aspects of life meant for grown-ups, not children, today the youngest child is exposed through the evening news to all of this. Tiny children see on TV people tortured or blown to bits in war-torn parts of the world, and they hear people joking about sexual topics on the latest and most popular sitcoms.

"Whoever causes one of these little ones who believe in me to sin, it would be better for him to have a great millstone fastened round his neck and to be drowned in the depth of the sea."[67]

The reaction of the Christian father must not be merely negative (although no television at all would be far better than uncontrolled television). To be truly effective, the parental response must flow from a united front, father and mother recognizing their positive responsibilities as teachers.

The training of a child requires more than a constant negation of the child's wrongdoing; it demands that the father be a positive influence in the home who must put forth positive efforts to educate those who belong to him. Wax is not molded merely by protecting it from melting; it must be worked upon with a conscious design. So in molding the young, we must ourselves know what we are training them to become.

Father-heroes instruct by example

Let us never forget that our primary duty is to help our children become disciples of the risen Christ. Secondarily, we must see to it

[67] Matt. 18:6.

that they will be able to take a place among the society of mature men and women. These two are not opposed; in fact, good citizenship in the wider community is a byproduct of mature Christian discipleship.

It goes without saying that the father who recognizes his vocation as a father as coming from Christ, who strives to pay special attention to Christ in those around him, who has brought the life of Christ as it is lived and renewed through the liturgical year into the home, and who exercises his prerogative to bless his children has already made progress in the proper education of his children. He is preparing that family atmosphere, which Pope Pius XII called for many years ago, "in which [the child] may open its eyes to light and its soul to life."

Still there is more that can be done. The birth of a child marks the start of that child's long training that will prepare him adequately for time and for eternity, and this training is to be shared by both father and mother, not left for the mother to do, as if it is none of the father's business. The father should be a teacher. Even as his other roles are not compartmentalized, but flow from the one person that he is, so his function as teacher is inextricably woven into the whole pattern of his existence, his way of being. When he goes to work, a father is still a father, and his roles as husband and father are more important than his role as worker.

Our role as teachers is not one that requires us to put a desk and chalkboard into a certain room and begin to prepare lectures for our children. No, our teaching is one that flows from the very beings we are and takes place, whether we wish it or not, in every contact between ourselves and our children. As fathers, we have in our homes growing youngsters whose larger questions may well be unasked questions, and to them we are unconsciously supplying and denying answers every day we live with them.

If we are to our secularized, "unchurched," or nonreligious neighbors Christianity incarnate, we are to our children much more. If our neighbor judges the Catholic Church by us, then our children get their picture of the entire world from us. Their norm for human relations will be our own relations with them, their mother, and others.

Verbally instructing our children to respect other people will have little effect if we tell them in other ways that we feel superior, intellectually and socially, to a particular group of people. On the other hand, to invite into our home as friends a family of another race, a family that may not be materially as well off as we are, or an elderly person who has no family living nearby, leaves an imprint upon our children's minds of how good it is to respect other people, regardless of their race, age, or material circumstances.

The example of our own lives will be the greatest teacher. Still, there are other means of education. In the home where Christ is welcome, where religion is a way of life and not another organization we belong to, the children themselves will provide ample opportunity for the father to give them some doctrinal training. A father should not wince at the questions of the young; childish though they be, they are important to the child, and the father can use them as an opportunity to forward the spiritual and intellectual growth of his children.

Be honest and positive about the mysteries of the Faith

A child's mind is undaunted by mystery. He will ask about the Incarnation, for instance, although not using that term. Years ago, one of our children, having received the information that God the Father was a spirit, therefore invisible, wanted to know why we could see Jesus. If Jesus was God, why wasn't He a spirit? Questions such as this call for accurate answers suitable to the mind of the child, and since they come without advance warning and with the child's insistence on an immediate answer, they keep Dad on his theological toes. Questions flow from the children's attendance at Mass, from the conversations they overhear, from the Bible stories they are read; they are not artificially stimulated. The young mind is an inquiring mind, trying to come to grips with the world into which it has been born. The task of the father is to keep that mind inquiring — not to cut off its questions — and yet to help it attain that grip on reality that it seeks.

When it comes to a choice between giving a correct answer that may not be fully understood or "begging the question" by some means, the former alternative is to be preferred. Beware of telling "pious fairy tales" — especially terrifying ones — to illustrate a point.

I know of one person who traces the crumbling of his faith to the little stories a teacher told him to impress upon his mind certain doctrines. Whether this teacher distinguished clearly in her own mind between the doctrine and the story is of no importance, for the child did not. The stories haunted him; he even had nightmares about them. When he grew old enough to see the stories as patently false, as "morality tales" without foundation, his faith suffered a crippling blow, and he left the Church.

On no account should we ever use God as a threat, as a bogeyman to frighten a child into obedience. Our constant emphasis should be upon God's love for us and upon our love for God. A child is naturally loving, seeks love, wants to be constantly assured of the fact that he is loved. The child requires all the love that can be given for the simple reason that a child senses his own dependence.

The world for a child is a world of giants and wonders, full of fearful mysteries that the child can meet with confidence only if he is confident of being loved. To instill in the child's mind the image of an awful monster called "God," greater even than parents, who is going to punish the child for every wrongdoing, is to cast love aside and fill his soul with fear. To root the child's relationship with God in fear may do untold damage to the future spiritual life of that child.

Exercise authority as does God the Father

One might mention the tremendous responsibility we, as fathers, have in regard to the image our children will have of God, of the Church, of all authority. How can a child understand the concept of a loving fatherhood of God if his own father is not loving? How can a child understand that he is free to go to the heavenly Father with problems and hopes if the earthly father, living in the child's own home, looks upon him as a nuisance?

We should remember that the way in which we exercise our authority at home will determine to a tremendous degree the way in which the child will react to all authority. If we fail to exercise our authority at all, if we are too indulgent, we shall do our children a grave injustice. Children need authority. When they do not find it at home, they will seek it elsewhere, in older companions, in the entertainment they see, the crowd they hang around with. The very totalitarian aspects of the youth subculture, and of youth gangs, is a commentary upon the lack of authority in the homes of our children and teenagers.

On the other hand, if we are arbitrary, unjust, and dictatorial, if we discipline for our own selfish ends, the child will soon rebel. And the child's rebellion may not stop with a mere rebellion against parental authority, but may express itself in a rebellion against all authority. At the least, the father who exercises his authority for his own selfish ends — every instruction a negative command or a prohibition — will soon find his children are strangers to him.

Such children will await their father's departure from the house so that they may live more exuberantly; they will dread his homecoming, and they will — if older — eagerly await the time when they can leave home. If he punishes them unjustly, in anger or out of proportion to their offense, he will find that their acquiescence to him is rooted in fear and their respect for him is a respect merely for his brute strength. His authority, his teachings, being selfish at root, will be obeyed only when he is present to enforce them.

The whole matter of wrongdoing and its punishment should be modeled after the way God deals with us. Should our children do wrong, we can attempt to find out if their wrongdoing was deliberate, accidental, or caused by some desire to do good; whether the child is sorry, willing to seek reconciliation in the case of a child's squabble, etc. Then, given the situation that the child has done something he knows to be wrong, we can introduce some logical consequence that fits the gravity of the situation.

Sometimes children can be allowed to exercise their own freedom in choosing which privilege they wish to forgo — dessert, story, television, allowance, and the like. But once the proper balance has been restored, the child should be made aware that he is once again on a good footing with all concerned. The child should not be harassed about the event, nor should the other children be allowed to taunt him about it.

Discipline means affirmation, too

It is the wise and patient father who can remind himself that young children do not possess full powers of reason, are not capable of the full exercise of free will. On the other hand, he must remember that human nature is far from perfect and that he must try to channel and train the will and the conscience of his children.

But our approach should here be more positive than negative. Praise for good motives and correct behavior is as necessary to our children as the correction of their bad decisions and choices. As someone once said, "Catch your children being good!"

Children crave attention, and they desire our approval. If we ignore them when their behavior is good, on the grounds that such behavior is expected, and give them attention only when they do wrong, they will sacrifice approval for attention.

The premise that his younger children see him as infallible should not make the father feel that he must live up to this impossible image. Our education of our children is an education for reality, and it is both unwise and unrealistic for the father to attempt to live up to the impossible concept, or image, of the perfect and all-knowing human being.

Even if the relationship of father and child somehow escaped being uneasy or inhuman, even if the father somehow was able to maintain the illusion of perfection for a time, the day of recognition of his father's clay feet could have a shattering effect upon the young child. On the other hand, the wise father, while remembering that to his children he is a hero, will — like the knights of old and those great heroes, the saints — remember to refer all things to God. A mistake, a wrong turn on some outing, a forgotten promise to bring home some ice cream, can be an occasion when the father can remind his children of his own humanity — of the fact that it is God alone who makes no mistakes and is not forgetful.

The relationship of fathers and children should be therefore a relationship in love, even as our relationship with God should be a relationship in love. God's command to children to honor their parents is not without its requirements upon parents; it is a command to them to live and to exercise their authority in such a way that they are worthy of honor and of love. They must be able to say with Christ, "My yoke is easy, and my burden is light."[68]

Allow children to make some decisions for themselves

It may be said of many parents that their children find their yoke a difficult yoke and their burden a heavy burden — probably because they look upon their children as a yoke and a burden neither sweet nor light. Such parents normally see everything their children request or desire as a threat to their "time" or "energy." They quickly lapse into the habit of saying no to all that a child might ask. They respond negatively without considering what the request is, what it may mean to the child, or whether it may be just as easy to say yes.

A child might ask to go to bed with one stocking on — because Deedle Deedle Dumpling in the Mother Goose book did — and the parent says no. There is no valid reason behind the denial, although in the child's mind, there was a real reason behind the request. The stocking will not be damaged or lost by being worn to bed, the child will be happy with it on, and there will be no great effort about finding it in the morning, should it have slipped off. The prompt no means the child has lost another opportunity to assert his own proper will.

One of the most important works of parents is the training of the child in the proper use of free will, and here is a case where the child might have been allowed that freedom of choice. While it is sometimes easier to say no without considering the request on its

[68] Matt. 11:30.

merits, it might be wiser and more worthwhile to say yes once in a while and, by this means, help the child toward independence of action.

This is not a call for a child-centered home in the sense that the children get everything they want — as is too often the case in the United States — but rather a suggestion that parents not overlook the self-training of their children in their own making of decisions and the acceptance of the consequences.

While my wife and I were the ones who decided whether our young children would have ice cream, the children got the opportunity to choose their flavor. If a dispute arose, Amy having chosen chocolate and Michael strawberry, but each wanting vanilla, as Mommy got, they were made to abide by their choices. This approach can be applied in innumerable situations, but the lesson is always the same: when freedom of choice is allowed, the consequences must be accepted.

Good training pays off in later years

As children grow older, the problem becomes more complex, is less susceptible of easy answers. What does a parent do when confronted by a seventeen-year-old full of the explosive force of adolescence, capable of going right or left, up or down? What can the father confronted by such a son or daughter do? Well, the question is wrongly phrased.

The fact of the matter is that if the father has not already done something, he is not going to be able to do anything now except pray earnestly. If, on the other hand, he has always maintained an open relationship with his child, if "business" and other selfishness have not clogged the channels of communication; if the son or daughter and the father have always loved and respected each other as persons, worthy of each other's love and respect, then the seventeen-year-old will have little trouble approaching Dad to discuss problems and plans.

Seventeen is an age of plans; adolescence is not just an age of rebellion. Adolescence is also the age of highest idealism, when young men and women feel they can climb the highest mountain, write the greatest book, remold the botched-up world that has been handed them. If we admit that the temptations and the forces at work in adolescence are powerful things, we must also admit that the idealism of adolescence is a beautiful thing.

But between the small child and the older adolescent is another and even more trying period. The first realization that some of his ideals are not common to all will cause the youngster to question — for he does not want to be different. Each father must seek how best to meet this crisis for the particular child. At certain ages, the desire to be one of the crowd is an intense, psychological necessity. There are many areas where this imitativeness may be allowed: to have the same kind of lunchbox, to get a certain style of haircut. The granting of such reasonable requests can help keep the child from feeling that the area of negation or the degree of difference is overwhelming. The wise father will strive not merely to negate this or that harmful public practice, but to replace it by a Christian and positive one.

Much depends upon the actual circumstances of the case and the temperament of the child, but the father might have recourse to the fact that *Christians are supposed to be different.* In fact, the crying shame of this world today is that too many Christians are indistinguishable from their nonreligious, even pagan, neighbors.

Sex education: the parents' right and duty

The issue of sexual instruction is one that troubles many fathers. It is naïve to think that the matter can be managed simply by having a parent-child talk on some specified day — "Now you can be told, my son (my daughter)" — or that the matter will be covered by a teacher at school or in a religious-education class. Sex education is not a matter of facts so much as it is an attitude toward one's own person and toward all created things.

There was no "sex problem" in this regard in the Middle Ages, because the Catholic Church at that time had a healthy attitude toward the human body. It took the Jansenism and Puritanism of the seventeenth and eighteenth centuries to change the attitudes, even of many otherwise good Catholics, toward the body, toward created things.

If we have brought up our children cognizant of the goodness of all created things, of the great dignity conferred upon the human body — including sexuality — when "the Word was made flesh," our task will not be so difficult. Too, if they have had each of their questions answered honestly and without a lot of blushing and stammering when it was asked, they will reach young adulthood with most of the fundamental facts. Again, the facts should be accurate, even though they must be simplified for the child. The child should neither be given a sense of shame about his or her genitals, nor should more information be given than is needed to satisfy the curiosity of the moment.

Instill a positive view of God's creation

The approach must always center upon the goodness of the body, of the goodness of sex, of the wonder that men and women can "help God" in creation. A father has no need to be embarrassed or fearful. When the occasions arise, when the child is curious about this or that aspect of sex, the parent has only to use common sense in transmitting to the child the truth concerning the excellent way in which God has made us.

The important thing is that the father himself know and accept the goodness and holiness of human sexuality. If he does, he will have little trouble bringing to his children the facts of human reproduction in a manner that will foster in them a respect for their own bodies and for the sacrament of marriage.

We found that allowing our children to watch their cat give birth to kittens inspired them with wonder. They knew that little kittens are kept inside their mother's "tummy" until they get big enough to live on the outside. There is no more normal and healthy way for children to learn the secrets of nature. Also, having seen their mother breast-feed the latest arrival, they learned what purpose breasts serve.

The child who has always received correct and adequate answers to his or her questions generally will not hesitate to ask further questions when they arise. Such a child's knowledge of the "facts of life" will grow with his or her own growth, keeping pace with natural curiosity and a developing ability to receive accurate information.

Education for this world and the next

For the child who is given a good home sex education throughout childhood, the time of adolescence and its concomitant turmoil will not be as difficult as for that child who has been taught that his body is shameful or dirty and who has discovered from some other youngster that his parents did "weird" things to bring him into the world. For the former child, all the new stirrings of his body and mind will find their proper place in life and in his understanding of God's goodness. For the latter child, adolescence can become a pit from which there may be no escape.

Our training of our children in spirituality and morality, a training that goes on all the time, is not merely an education for

eternity. By giving our children a religious formation, we are training them in a way that prepares them to cope adequately with the
conditions of life on earth. The knowledge of Christ can give people hope in the face of the perils of war and terrorism. The teachings of the Catholic Church and the experience of the sacraments
can bring order and peace to this earth. Not only is there no
conflict between being a good citizen and a good Christian, but St.
Augustine could say: "Let those who declare the teaching of
Christ to be opposed to the welfare of the state furnish us with an
army of soldiers such as Christ says soldiers ought to be; let them
give us subjects, husbands, wives, parents, children, masters, ser-
vants, kings, judges, taxpayers, and tax-gatherers who live up to
the teachings of Christ; and then let them dare assert that Christian doctrine is harmful to the state. Rather, let them not hesitate
one moment to reclaim that doctrine, rightly observed, the greatest safeguard of the state."

If we bring up our children formed in the image of Christ, we
will not only have brought them up ready for the battles of this age
in which we live, but we will have given to the world some good
citizens, people who are a credit to humanity.

Give children a sense of history

Children enter history through the family into which they are
born, and people in the United States are losing, if they have not
already lost, their sense of family. Even I, born prior to World War
II, know nothing of either of my grandparents, for instance, save
one hazy recollection of my mother's mother visiting our home
when I was a child. She never visited us again, and she died a few
years later.

I think that in this I am typical of most of my generation, not to
mention many members of the younger generations, as well. Many

of us have no real sense of family lineage, no blood lines, no historical feeling. Personally, I miss this knowledge; I feel it as a lack within me, and I am nostalgic for what I feel is my rightful heritage. I hope that I provided my children, all now grown, with that knowledge of which I (and this is not meant to impute blame upon anyone) was deprived.

Through human relationships, mementoes, photos, and stories, we tried to awaken in our children an awareness of the family as something more than the people with whom they lived. Perhaps we helped them to recognize family for what it is: a living entity that extends back through time and space and forward into the future. If they have gained this sense of family, perhaps as they begin families of their own, they will come to an appreciation of their role as bearers of a culture and of a tradition, a Christian culture and a Christian tradition.

For children to feel at home in the world, it is essential that they have a home in the world. In order for them to recognize their familial ties with all humankind, it is necessary for them to have familial ties with people outside their immediate family. I think it is no less important for them to become familiar with their grandparents, if only from secondary sources, as they are with their parents and will be with their children and their children's children.

The person of wisdom is the one with a sense of history. When such a person not only looks to the past and knows whence he came, but looks to the future and knows where he is going, that person is making that first step toward the knowledge that leads to wholeness and holiness.

Give your children a sense of wonder
Our teaching at home is not only — or even mainly — a teaching of facts, however. It is the handing on to the child of a

whole view, a Christian view, of the universe. This is not so difficult a task as it may at first seem; the wonder of a child at creation is in itself a holy thing.

This sense of wonder is a real, profound awe at the existence of concrete beings. The child, in this sense, is a metaphysician, and his wonder is kept ever fresh by each new discovery made concerning the self or the world. In paying attention to creation, in rejoicing in creating things, the child is like St. Francis of Assisi[69] offering a prayer to God.

It is tragic that the sense of wonder, the sense of mystery before God's handiwork, is so soon snuffed out in our hectic world, so often immersed under the tide of artificial distractions, amusements, and busyness.

The wonder of a child at existence ought not be crushed either, by any too-doctrinaire approach to the realities of faith, morals, or the world of human relationships. Especially, a child's spirit should not be crushed by the negative-formula approach that is loaded with an endless list of all the things not to do in order to be a good Christian.

Christianity is not a set of prohibitions, nor is it a list of negative statements; rather, it is an explosive affirmation of existence, of the goodness of created things, of the glorious destiny that awaits people who have learned to love their neighbor for the love of God.

Children can be our heroes, too

The task is not easy. The burden is not light. The obligation is grave. The responsibility is as great as any that a person can hold:

---

[69] St. Francis of Assisi (1182-1226), founder of the Franciscan Order.

the responsibility to raise up rightly a new life for God. But God has promised those joined together in the sacrament of marriage all of the help necessary for them to fulfill their vocations. (In this regard, however, many parishes could be doing more than they are to support married couples and parents.) The rearing of our children is one of the main tasks of our vocation, so God is with us in this holy work.

Children are themselves carriers of God's self-gift for their parents. Indeed, in one sense, children are the models for parents. To look at a young child is to see what purity of heart it is we are asked by Christ to strive for: "Truly, I say to you, unless you turn and become like children, you will never enter the kingdom of Heaven. Whoever humbles himself like this child, he is the greatest in the kingdom of Heaven."[70]

The almost tangible holiness of little children is a holiness we should do all in our power to protect and nurture as our children grow up, a holiness we can look to as a reminder of what God wants of us. The obedience we ask and expect of our children is the obedience that God asks and expects of us. Their innocence, their directness and honesty — that is what God wants of us. Their dependence upon us for all their needs is but a tiny image of our dependence upon God, the Father of all.

If we are, in fact, images of the world and of God to our children, they should be for us images of what we are to become if we wish to enter the kingdom of Heaven. The teacher who has not the humility to learn from his pupils is not a teacher at all.

[70] Matt. 18:3-4.

Chapter 6

The Father as Breadwinner

"It has always been the duty of Christian married partners, but today it is the greatest part of their apostolate to manifest and prove by their own way of life the indissolubility and sacredness of the marriage bond, strenuously to affirm the right and duty of parents and guardians to educate children in a Christian manner, and to defend the dignity and lawful autonomy of the family. They and the rest of the faithful, therefore, should cooperate with men of good will to ensure the preservation of these rights in civil legislation and to make sure that governments give due attention to the needs of the family regarding housing, the education of children, working conditions, social security, and taxes; and that in policy decisions affecting migrants, their right to live together as a family should be safeguarded."

Decree on the Apostolate of the Laity, no. 11

G ive us this day our daily bread," we pray to our Father in Heaven, and as we look to God, so children look to their parents. The father of the family is normally a "breadwinner." One of his primary responsibilities is to provide for his family those basic necessities of life symbolized by bread, "the staff of life." The family owes to the labors of the parents all these things without which civilized existence would be impossible: food, clothing, and shelter.

In less complex times, the almost complete reliance of the family upon the labors of the father and mother was more visible; more often than not, the father tilled the soil while the mother ran the household, and together they managed life on the family farm. If the father labored arduously with rude tools, if for long hours in the hot sun he sweated over the soil, he was rewarded with the pleasure of contemplating a land made fruitful by his own calloused hands, and he could dip those hands into the freshly ground wheat before his wife kneaded it into loaves that would be broken at their meal. Both parents and children could see the direct relationship between the labor of the parents and their daily life: "Give us this day our daily bread."

Changing times mean a new role for the breadwinner

Today, the concept of the father as the sole supporter of a family, which dominated the scene (at least among white middle-class families) for as long as twenty years following the Second World War, has been dislocated. In many cases, the mother and wife contributes as much as the father and husband to the support of the family. But even in those families where the father continues to assume full responsibility as provider, his task has undergone a change.

Instead of winning his bread from a soil enriched with his sweat, the average father sweats elsewhere: in an office, behind the wheel of a bus or a truck, in front of a lathe, or at the keyboard of a computer. He works to earn the money that will purchase the "bread" — the material necessities to sustain his family. In short, he has ceased to be a breadwinner in the literal sense of the term and has become a wage earner. Between the labors of the father and mother and the food on the table stands the "wage" that they have earned, the money they supply. And it is here that danger confronts the contemporary family.

That the father sweats in a place foreign, usually, to the gaze of his wife and children means that his responsibility in contributing his part to the family's needs becomes less visible (as does his wife's, in the instances where she works outside the home, too).

The family can lose sight of the truly vital link between the father's labors and the food on the table, for he neither grew nor harvested it, although frequently today he may have gone to the store to buy it. Perhaps only subconsciously, but often quite openly, the father is looked upon by his family as one who helps to pay the bills. All too often he himself sees his paternal role only in this limited way.

"I don't know what she wants of me," one man cried out toward the end of his tale of marital strife. "I've given her and the kids everything. I'm breaking my back to do it — just meeting the payments is killing me, but I don't complain. The doctor tells me to slow down, but how can I slow down? Each month there are all those bills to pay" — he looked up — "and they get paid! She and the kids must think I've got a magic wand, but they're killing the magician."

Another man, whose wife was divorcing him after fourteen years of marriage, said, "We had nothing when we were married. Now she's got her own car, the best of everything. If she wanted anything for herself or the kids, all she had to do was write a check."

A third husband and father complained that his wife was brow-beating him to death: "We both work full-time, so I understand that she's tired when she gets home. But she keeps nagging me about helping more around the house. Hey, I'm tired, too!"

The first of these men had allowed his family to thrust him into the role of bill-payer, and he did not know how to get out; the second had failed even to glimpse that his fatherhood involved any more responsibility, any involvement more profound than that of a supplier of material wants; the third thought it unfair that his wife, who works full-time just as he does, would want him to shoulder more of the household duties.

Not by bread — or "stuff" — alone

It does not take much insight to see that if the responsibility of the father is only to contribute to the material welfare of his family, then the father of a family could easily be replaced by a bank account or a trust fund. But Christ has warned us that it is not by bread alone that people live.

No one argues the fact that it is a primary duty of a father to contribute to the material welfare of his family. But this responsibility must be viewed in its proper perspective. The true material needs of a family are few. In the United States, most people would not find the task of meeting those needs beyond their powers. Yet the basic worry of family men in the United States seems to be a concern over material things, and financial problems are a major cause of marital strife. Too often, such financial problems are due to a confusion between true needs and the false needs aroused by advertisers.

"What man of you, if his son asks him for bread, will give him a stone? Or if he asks for a fish, will give him a serpent?"[71] What man would do such a thing? Where is the man who hands his sons stones instead of bread? Is he not, perhaps, that one quoted above who gave his family the stones of manufactured "stuff," bank accounts, blank checks for material purposes? Isn't he the man who is "too busy" with his work to eat even the main meal of the day with his family? Isn't the man who is so engrossed in earning money outside of the home that he doesn't know what is going on within its walls another who brings home stones?

The father who thrusts the religious formation of his children entirely onto the shoulders of his wife and Catholic-school teachers or parish catechists has handed his son the stone that may break his spiritual spine as he grows up thinking of religion as mainly for women and girls. The father who is too embarrassed to say grace at mealtimes has handed his children a stone — the stone of a sin we might call "fear of human opinion." But all of us are guilty of giving our children stones instead of bread. How many times have we come home burdened with the day's fatigues and worries and given to our children nothing but the stone of our cold presence, refusing to open ourselves to them, to the healing laughter of their innocence? No, if we examine our consciences, few of us could claim never to have committed this crime.

[71] Matt. 7:9-10.

But how many no longer see the difference between stones and bread? These are the fathers who think of their parenthood as a material duty rather than a spiritual one, who believe that as long as the bills are paid, they are meeting their responsibility. Today's news reports of juvenile drug use, teenage pregnancies, adolescent suicides, brutal family atrocities, and the like all testify that many men are handing their children not the bread that only a true father can give, but the stones of that anonymous man who helps to pay the bills, the man who could be replaced by a trust fund.

Spiritual welfare is more important than material

To meet real needs, to feed the hungry, clothe the naked, shelter the homeless: yes, our obligation to others in charity is a serious obligation in justice to our family. We are morally bound to contribute all that we can to provide for them. But to exert our powers, to exhaust ourselves in the accumulation of money, to strive after all the unneeded luxuries and self-indulgent trivia held out by the advertising industry, and to neglect the human and spiritual welfare of those to whom we have bound ourselves: this is to follow the path of the Tempter.

When the Tempter approaches Jesus in Matthew's Gospel, he says, "If you are the Son of God, command these stones to become loaves of bread."[72] This is a double-barreled temptation: a temptation to pride and to greed. Satan asks Jesus to assert His divine power in a vain display, but he also asks Jesus, who has been fasting for forty days, to forgo His reliance upon His Father in Heaven and to provide food for Himself. It is this very temptation to ostentation and to a lack of trust in our heavenly Father that causes many fathers to devote their energies almost entirely to earning money.

[72] Matt. 4:3.

Such men have allowed themselves to be seduced by the same temptation that Jesus thrusts aside with the words "It is written, 'Man shall not live by bread alone, but by every word that proceeds from the mouth of God.' "[73]

Jesus does not hesitate to multiply loaves and fishes in abundance when a hungry multitude needs nourishment; but He gives us an example of trust in God and the rejection of proud display. It is an example little heeded in contemporary society where men (and women) avid for the amassing and display of wealth allow their work as breadwinners to cut them off from their families and from God. Sadly, if a man allows his job to do one of these things, it will eventually do the other.

Such men bring home not bread, but stones.

The best thing we give children is ourselves

We read about these unfortunate fathers in our newspapers every day, and we see them on evening news programs on television. Sometimes we see them in criminal courtrooms where their teenager is on trial, their grief-stricken faces asking, "Where did I go wrong?" Often they beg the judge and the world to believe that "I've given him everything."

But is not that admission really an answer to their question? In giving their children everything, weren't they doing wrong? "Everything" — if it means only everything of a material nature — is not enough. In fact, everything is too little as long as it does not include a relationship in love.

To give things is not to give love. The things we give to others can serve only as outward signs, symbolic expressions, and often tragically fragile ones, of the ineffable inner commitment to the

---

[73] Matt. 4:4.

good of the other, which we call love. To give love is to give of ourselves. To love is to exist for the other, and the greatest love is to surrender our lives for the good of the one we love.

"The tongue of the nursling cleaves to the roof of its mouth for thirst; the children beg for food, but no one gives it to them," the book of Lamentations cries.[74] We can accept this description for those unfortunate enough to have a father who "gave them everything" but forgot the "one thing necessary." The starvation of the body that the prophet depicted is but a pale image of that starvation of spirit that is behind every case we read about of children who run away from home or who are rejected by their parents, who end up in crime, drugs, and prostitution. Our newspapers are filled with reports of a world starving for love.

A consumerist society will never find happiness

We are human beings, and we live in history. The world we inhabit today is a world enraptured by sparkling, gleaming, intriguing "stuff." We are the target of a daily, ever-so-enticing attack on our wills. An hour does not pass without bringing, in many forms, countless blatant suggestions that this or that product will make us happy, successful, or secure. There is the underlying suggestion, of course, that without this, whatever it is, we will be unhappy, unsuccessful, and insecure. Billions of dollars a year are spent in the endeavor to convince us that our peace will come with the latest products on the market.

Money, battening on our technological civilization, has grown from a mere medium of exchange, a token we use to obtain things we need, to a thing sought after for its own sake. It has ceased being a means and has become an end. Previously, in a non-money

[74] Lam. 4:4.

society, people working the soil were limited by the extent of their own energies — one person can do only so much work — and by the horizon of their own needs. Any excess of the fields that could not be bartered off for other necessities would spoil.

The very cycle of nature held greed in check. Sheep can be sheared and a crop can be harvested only when nature has readied them for the human hand. Even if a family could afford the time away from work, they would be insane to build a home twice as large as they needed; and to burden themselves with more horses than they had a use for would have been sheer stupidity.

The advent of money and a moneyed economy changed this, removed this natural barrier to human acquisitiveness. Money, having no contact with nature, being in fact an unnatural thing, could be gathered without cease; it did not spoil; it did not wait upon the seasons; it could be gained, counted, banked, exchanged, and otherwise manipulated at all hours of the day or night. Gathering interest, it could even multiply itself!

There is little likelihood — barring the absolute devastation that would result from a nuclear war — that our technological society will abolish itself, nor do sensible people ask us to turn back the pages of history and deny the many advantages that we enjoy but our ancestors never fancied. Idyllic daydreams of a "simpler life" often exclude the harsher aspects of past ages.

Still, the fact that we enjoy advantages that our fathers and mothers did not know is no reason to deny that we face challenges and problems they did not face. Oftentimes, these are made more difficult because they present themselves not as problems and challenges, but only as facts of our daily existence.

One such fact is the terrible tendency of the father of the family to look upon himself as the materialistic Marx (and I don't mean Groucho) looked upon him: a mere producer and consumer of goods. Another tendency is the thoughtlessness that attributes to money a power it does not have: the power to fill the abyss created in the human soul when love is absent.

If we give our children only the material goods of this world — no matter how "high-tech" they may be — we shall starve them to death, and, before God, we shall answer for our crime. Jesus, taking on His lap a little child, says that "whoever receives one such child in my name receives me." He continues, "but whoever causes one of these little ones who believe in me to sin, it would be better for him to have a great millstone fastened round his neck and to be drowned in the depth of the sea."[75]

It might be time for Christian fathers to examine their consciences, ponder the attitudes they have adopted from the society in which they live, and see whether they really want to pass such ideals on to their children.

Dependence on God is the key to poverty of spirit

The Christian father should remember that, although he is a man involved in human history, a man caught up in time, human history was fractured two thousand years ago by the Son of God, who entered time in order to redeem it. Our human history is now sacred history, for Christ is involved in it. In his marriage, the Christian father knows that he mirrors the relationship of Christ with His people, the Church. And even as the Church through Baptism brings new members into union with Christ, so, too, does the Christian father cooperate with God in the creation of new members for the Body of Christ.

We have spoken elsewhere of the educative and priestly aspects of the father's vocation. It should be unnecessary to point

[75] Matt. 18:5-6.

out that all of these aspects of fatherhood overlap, that the father is one person and not many, and that our arbitrary division of his single role as father of the family is made solely in order to penetrate better the mystery of his fatherhood. It naturally follows that much of what was said concerning the power of the father's own example and the real penetration of the life of the Church into the home will help us here in meeting the call of our children for bread, in fulfilling our duties as fathers.

But one thing should be underscored. The best defense against evil is an offense. If evil would use all the weapons of modern technology to stamp upon us the image of modern technological humankind, then we must strive to attain in our own lives that spirit of Christian poverty which Christ counsels us to. We must seek true and pure poverty of spirit, which is rooted in trusting dependence upon God.

We must remember at all times that the bread we have on our tables is there by the grace of God. Upon all the goods with which God might reward our labors we must seek His blessing. No family meal should be consumed that has not first been the subject of prayerful thanks to the One who gave it to us.

The family table is an image of the table of the Eucharist. Even as at table a family shares the same life-giving substance, so at the Mass all the members of the Body of Christ partake of Him who called Himself "the life." Even as the food and drink parents provide help the family to grow in health and strength, so our Father in Heaven gives us His Son, who says in John's Gospel: "He who eats my flesh and drinks my blood abides in me and I in him."[76] "For my flesh is food indeed, and my blood is drink indeed."[77]

---

[76] John 6:56.
[77] John 6:55.

True Christian poverty does not mean destitution. Some of the poorest people materially have not the spirit of poverty. Neither does true Christian poverty mean that one must look upon the things of this world as evil — which would be the sin of more than one Christian heresy and an implicit denial of the fullness of the Incarnation. Rather, the Christian father remains detached from the fruits of his labors. He remembers that these things are not important in themselves and that people do not need things to be happy, that happiness is to be found in doing the will of God.

The freedom that comes from such detachment is but a dim reflection of the freedom that Christ Himself displays in the Gospels. Jesus sits at the tables of the rich; He defends the use of the costliest oils in the anointing of His feet; He is accused of associating with tax collectors and prostitutes; but in Matthew's Gospel He also says of Himself: "Foxes have holes and birds of the air have nests, but the Son of man has nowhere to lay His head."[78]

Most Christians are not called upon to renounce the ownership of property, but all are called upon to keep their hearts and wills free from attachment to "stuff," mere possessions. "Therefore, I tell you, do not be anxious about your life, what you shall eat or what you shall drink, nor about your body, what you shall put on."[79] "Truly, I say to you, it will be hard for a rich man to enter the kingdom of Heaven."[80] "Children, how hard it is for those who trust in riches to enter the kingdom of God!"[81] Again and again in the Gospels we find Jesus returning to the same theme: In order to enter the kingdom of God, one must remember: "No servant can

---

[78] Matt. 8:20.
[79] Matt. 6:25.
[80] Matt. 19:23.
[81] Mark 10:24.

serve two masters; for either he will hate the one and love the other, or he will be devoted to the one and despise the other. You cannot serve God and mammon."[82]

Place the Giver above His gifts

Years ago, during one of the great California forest fires, a young executive left his office to race to his foothill home and rescue what he might. Along the highway, where the road turned off into the hills, he met his wife. She informed him that the fire was still a few hundred yards from their barn, but their home was sure to be destroyed. She went back to the house with her husband, who told her to let out the dog and the cats from the house while he ran to free the horses from their stables.

When his wife returned to his side, she asked, "What shall we save now?" And the man said, "Nothing." Back on the highway, the man explained that as he drove home, he had been anxiously cataloging in his mind all of the possessions that he must rescue from the blaze. Before reaching his wife, however, he had decided that they had a duty to the living creatures, the horses, the dog, and the cats, but that all the rest was unimportant. "We don't need things to be happy," he told his wife. "We must not lose our freedom to things."

So the couple drove back to the city, took a room in a hotel, and waited for the fire to be brought under control. When they returned to their homesite, they found that the wind had averted the fire only a few yards from their home. Their house and all of their possessions were intact. "Perhaps if I had tried to save those things," the man said later, "I would have lost them all — God's way of showing me their unimportance."

[82] Luke 16:13.

One wishes more people could see the truth this man saw, could recognize that while material things are good, they are gifts of God, and the gifts are not to be placed above the Giver. They are tokens of God's love, but who would prefer the token to the Lover?

What bride and groom, showing their wedding rings, would not consider insane the question of which they loved most: their rings or each other? All that we have, our very existence itself, we have as the free gift of God. All that is given, is given to bring us closer to God's love for us.

Indeed, we must even be willing to consider that our material benefits are the result of our interactions with sheer accident! After all, God loves with an endless love countless people in the world who have far fewer possessions and "creature comforts" than we. Certainly we may not attribute their material poverty to a lack of love for them on God's part.

And yet, even in Jesus' day people missed the fundamental fact, preferred the gift to the Giver. In the Gospel of John, the multitude that Jesus has fed with five barley loaves and two fish the day before seeks Him out. And when the crowd finds Jesus, he says to them: "Truly, truly, I say to you, you seek me not because you saw signs, but because you ate your fill of the loaves."[83]

The crowd had accepted the gift and missed its meaning, had failed to understand the spiritual message behind the "sign," had not seen this prodigious event as an example of God's goodness, His gift-giving, His "bounty." Instead, they accepted the bread as mere physical nourishment, and He who had filled their stomachs they wanted to make their king. Human nature has not changed since.

[83] John 6:26.

Bread from Heaven: perfect sign of God's Providence

We live in the midst of crowds who do not know enough to thank God for the food that He has given them, and who allow the material goods of this life to form a wall between them and their neighbors near and far, rather than to be a constant reminder of God's solicitude. The words that Jesus directs to the crowd are an attempt to correct this attitude. "Do not labor for the food which perishes, but for the food that endures to eternal life."[84]

The entire sixth chapter of John's Gospel should be read; it is too lengthy to quote in full here. It reminds those of us who are busy about the work of earning the daily bread for our tables that this natural bread, like the bread that Moses gave, the manna in the desert, is not "the living bread which came down from Heaven."[85] Jesus in the Fourth Gospel says: "Your fathers ate the manna in the wilderness, and they died. This is the bread which comes down from Heaven, that a man may eat of it and not die."[86]

As breadwinners for our families, we should meditate often upon these words and this chapter of the Gospel of John. The bread that we win, that natural bread that graces our tables, important as it is to the bodily health of ourselves and our families, should be for us a symbol, even as the manna was, of "the true bread from Heaven."[87] And that bread is the risen Christ. "For the bread of God is that which comes down from Heaven, and gives life to the world."[88]

[84] John 6:27.
[85] John 6:51.
[86] John 6:49-51.
[87] John 6:32.
[88] John 6:33.

Chapter 7

The Father as Saint

Married couples and Christian parents should follow their own proper path (to holiness) by faithful love. They should sustain one another in grace throughout the entire length of their lives. They should imbue their offspring, lovingly welcomed as God's gift, with Christian doctrine and the evangelical virtues. In this manner, they offer all men the example of unwearying and generous love; in this way they build up the brotherhood of charity; in so doing, they stand as the witness and cooperators in the fruitfulness of Holy Mother Church; by such lives, they are a sign and a participation in that very love, with which Christ loved His Bride and for which He delivered Himself up for her."

Dogmatic Constitution on the Church, no. 41

The Great Adventurers of the modern world": with these words Charles Péguy, the great French Catholic poet of the early twentieth century, honored the fathers of families. Péguy was killed in the first of the modern world's global wars, but if he were alive today, he would probably feel the need to underscore his statement.

What soldier of fortune faces a greater challenge than that confronted by the father, in partnership with his wife, navigating the ship of the family through the currents of modern life? Erupting from the depths of life's sea, raging storms — seen only as warnings on the barometer in Péguy's day — now crash full against the seams of the family ark, tearing at its white sails of holiness, pounding against its bulwarks that are the unity and indissolubility of marriage. If at any given time the parents underestimate the danger or fail to respond adequately to the challenge, the ship may founder.

"The Great Adventurers of the modern world," indeed. And called to an adventure of no little importance: the pitting of ourselves against all the enemies of fatherhood; the warding off of all the daily advances of a multibillion-dollar advertising industry devoted to making us and our children avaricious, lustful, and proud — all of this, yes, but more. Ours is not only a defensive action; we must at the same time take the offensive. We fight against storms, but for the sake of arriving at our destination. The enemy without must be held off while each day sees new attacks of the enemy within.

Fatherhood is a call to daily holiness

If we, as lay Catholics, have the mission of bringing a Christian witness to our society; if we, as the fathers of families, have the obligation of nourishing holiness in our homes, we must become Christ-like; we must be real-world saints. For those who think of holiness in terms of officially canonized saints, or as the special province of those who have been called to the vowed religious life, this blunt statement may come as a surprise. Yet the words of Christ in Matthew's Gospel are even more forceful: "You, therefore, must be perfect, just as your heavenly Father is perfect."[89]

These words are not spoken to any individual selected from among the Apostles, nor even to the Apostles alone, Matthew says, but to "great crowds,"[90] a multitude so large that "He went up on the mountain"[91] in order to speak to them. There can be no denying that we are included in these "great crowds," that Jesus' words are for all people throughout all time. Each of us is called to a life of holiness that has no limits.

Some dismiss this call as unrealistic, asking, "How can I hope to achieve holiness when I'm so caught up in daily cares, when the children demand so much time, when the job leaves me completely fatigued?" Others may try to live the life of a monk with one part of their being and the life of a layperson committed to worldly chores with the other. Such an endeavor can lead a man to

[89] Matt. 5:48.
[90] Matt. 4:25.
[91] Matt. 5:1.

look upon those with whom he lives and works as so many obstacles in his path to God, as hindrances to his contemplation, and as distractions from his prayers.

Such men often begin to evidence a real impatience with others that expresses itself in self-righteous indignation. In most cases, they soon give up the struggle and join that group of men who have decided beforehand that holiness is impossible under the circumstances of their lives.

Some few persist, though, determined to succeed in spite of family or friends; steeling their hearts, they seal themselves off in their own rooms for hours at a time for prayer and contemplation and think they are succeeding in their spiritual life when they have gotten their family to keep quiet during such times.

The trials of domestic life make us holy

What all these individuals fail to realize is that the call to sanctity is one conditioned to their state in life: for fathers of families, it is in and through our fatherhood that we are to achieve our fullest holiness. Not in spite of marriage and our family will we become holy, but because of them. Our parental work, when performed in Christ, is our holy work, as holy a work as that of any celibate religious who works full-time in a parish ministry, cares for the poor, houses the homeless, or prays unceasingly in a cloister.

There is particular relevance for us, as fathers, in that incident which occurs in the Gospel of Mark: "And He sat down and called the Twelve; and He said to them, 'If anyone would be first, he must be last of all and servant of all.' "[92]

It is in and through the experiences of marriage, and in the labors of rearing a family, of welcoming God in the children we are

[92] Mark 9:35.

given, that we are to advance in the spiritual life. We were called to the vocation of Christian marriage. We are laypeople, and our care for our families, our domestic churches, is at the very heart of the life of the Church as a whole. Our daily work, whatever it may be, our bill-paying and our bedtime reading, is holy already; there is no need for us to think up ways to make it holy. It remains for us only to remember the holiness of all that we are about, to recognize and appreciate this fact and celebrate it in ways natural to family life.

God uses our failures to purify and strengthen us

This is the glorious adventure upon which we are embarked. Yet, how often we fail! Our resolutions seem so quickly shattered under one or another of the day's poundings. We are human beings, not angels; we are the sons and daughters of the fallen Adam and Eve, and we ache with the bruises of all our own falls. "Out of the depths I cry to Thee, O Lord . . ."[93] and cry we must, but we must not become discouraged, for our major conquest is intended to be ourselves.

All of the pounding to which we are submitted on the anvil of our daily lives is intended to form us in the image of Christ. Like iron that, to be shaped, must be heated and pounded, heated and pounded, so we are heated with the flames of daily life and shaped by the life of God in us.

"It is for discipline that you have to endure," the letter to the Hebrews says. "God is treating you as sons; for what son is there whom his father does not discipline? . . . He disciplines us for our good, that we may share His holiness. For the moment all discipline seems painful rather than pleasant; yet it yields peaceful fruit

[93] Ps. 130:1.

of righteousness to those who have been trained by it. Therefore lift your drooping hands and strengthen your weak knees, and make straight paths for your feet, that what is lame may not be put out of joint but rather be healed. Strive for peace with all men, and for the holiness without which no one will see the Lord."[94]

In Christ, even our failures become a source of grace when we accept them in imitation of His humility and courage; even our anxieties become a path to holiness when we ally them with His sufferings. All that we do and say, if it is done and said in Christ, is done and said well, for true wellness is life in Christ.

Fathers need the Cross as well as the Resurrection

There are many who would not classify themselves among the unbelievers; indeed, they would be indignant at the suggestion, so comfortably are they ensconced in their religious formalism. Yet the New Testament saves its harshest words not for unbelievers standing outside the Church, but for those warming themselves within: "I know your works: you are neither cold nor hot. Would that you were cold or hot! So, because you are lukewarm, and neither cold nor hot, I will spew you out of my mouth."[95]

As a Christian, the father of the family cannot be mediocre. He cannot be satisfied with being a Christian in name only or on Sundays only. He may not thrust aside the uncomfortable standard that Christ raises: the standard of the inseparability of the Cross and the Resurrection. Those who preach a Christianity without the Cross, or promote "New Age" ideas designed to lead to a joy apart from sorrow, miss a basic message of the Gospel: we must pick up our cross and follow Christ in our daily life, or ours is no

[94] Heb. 12:7, 10-14.
[95] Rev. 3:15-16.

Christian life at all. (Indeed, those who blithely remove the crucifix from Catholic churches announcing, "The Resurrection is what it's all about" are only kidding themselves; they are out of touch with the real world that people live in, and they do a deep injustice to the message of Christ.)

The Christian father must look before him to the ideal set up by Christ, and then he must look to the means Christ gives him in order that he may overcome obstacles to his growth in holiness. Against those obstacles the contemporary father does not need merely to be a "nice guy" but to be a man of faith, hope, and love.

The world's hardships must drive us to deeper faith

How especially necessary these are today! How, without genuine faith, hope, and love, can a man be expected to stand up against the modern world's frontal assaults on the family? We live in a society that in many ways is anti-child. Commodity merchants and the media encourage a "generation gap" mentality — central to which is the existence of a "youth subculture" — that strains even further the normally sensitive parent/child relationship. Enormous pressure is placed on parents to strive for material "security"; billions of dollars are spent inculcating the "insurance mentality" that looks to the future with dread.

The ferment going on through our society and the world as a result of the constantly accelerating rate of social change; the attacks on "institutional religion"; the increasing acceptance of the "drug culture" and divorce; the rising tide of violence and the acceptance of abortion and euthanasia by many people: all are factors that make almost daily demands on a father's trust in God and his willingness to be guided by the Gospel and Catholic Tradition.

It is in a time such as our own that faith is truly revealed. For the times make continual demands on the Christian to reaffirm faith not only in prayer, but in acceptance of God's will and the willingness to speak out both by words and by deeds of faith in Christ.

Confronted by the possibility of terrorism, nuclear war, and ecological disaster, as well as the ever-present threat of drugs and the trivialization of sex; facing a world ripped by violence, atrocities, and genocide; and knowing his children will enter this world — only the father who has faith in God and a lively hope can overcome the tendency to despair. Only such a man is truly ready for the adventure of fatherhood.

Despite the deathly secularistic environment, despite the immensely more difficult task of protecting his children from such influences, the modern father — well aware that he cannot succeed without God's help — must hope in God's goodness that He will provide the means for him and his children to obtain eternal life, beginning here and now. This confident belief in God on the part of the father will be one of the strongest reasons that his family will find it easy to believe in Him.

Love validates a father's sacrifice of self

Faith, hope, and love: without these no father could long succeed in meeting the challenges of his calling, "but the greatest of these is love."[96] The often-quoted thirteenth chapter of Paul's first letter to the Corinthians should be reread frequently by all parents. It tells us that the faith which moves mountains is worthless without love. It tells us that although we devote all our time and energy to feeding the poor, it is meaningless unless we have love. Paul does not hesitate to say that although we submit to being burned at the stake for our Faith, it merits us nothing if love is lacking.

[96] 1 Cor. 13:13.

On the other hand, the most humble act done with love manifests the presence of the risen Christ. Love transforms, transfigures all. All Christians know this, but the father of a family has special cause to meditate and act upon it, since the greatest demands his daily life will make upon him will be demands upon his love.

In a sense, the father of a family has given himself away, gone to the stake, allowed himself to be consumed. But if he lacks love, if his giving is the cause of impatience, if it is rooted in self-interest or pride, if sacrifice becomes the cause of private brooding or regret, then neither his giving nor his sacrifice count for much.

The father of a family has an unparalleled opportunity to root his entire life in his love of God. His heart can rejoice at the mere thought of each new child who, through him, will come to share the goodness of life. What, in a man without love, is seen as an impingement upon his freedom, an intrusion upon his privacy, a diminishing of his self, is seen by the man who loves God as an opportunity for showing forth that love.

Love makes our homes an evangelical witness

Moreover, his recognition of the way in which his family impinges upon him, far from being the source of any malice toward those who are a drain upon his resources and time, is seen as the way in which he is being transformed in Christ. Such a man takes joy in receiving the living souls entrusted to him with patience and kindness, remembering the words of Jesus: "I say to you, whatever you did for one of these least brothers of mine, you did for me."[97]

Our homes become schools of love for all who live there, a love that of its nature radiates outward, first to the receiving of all

---

[97] Matt. 25:40.

guests as Christ and then to the meeting with equal love those who lack sympathy with our beliefs and our way of life. We can will the good of all our enemies. All those who are dedicated to ideals destructive of all we hold dear have a call upon our prayers.

Perhaps through the love we hold for such people, the example we set for them in Christ, we will one day be privileged to hear the words that St. Augustine addressed to St. Ambrose:[98] "I was not convinced by your arguments, but by the great love you showed me."

True poverty means spiritual wealth and freedom

The traditional "evangelical counsels," too — poverty, chastity, and obedience — also have a place in the life of the adventurer for Christ. If we are all called to be holy, then we are called upon to follow, in keeping with our vocation in life, these Gospel-based "counsels."

Because poverty, as such, is linked in the American mind with destitution, it is rarely understood or recommended; but Christian poverty is not destitution. Nothing less than a radical spirit of poverty or simplicity of life can cut a path of liberty through the jungle of commercialism in which we find ourselves. What less than a slicing away of the entangling undergrowth of senseless luxuries will allow us to find a sane balance for our daily lives? The most compelling need of our day, especially in the United States, a need more urgent than ever before in history, is for families who will re-enthrone the Lady Poverty of St. Francis of Assisi in their hearts.

Such families will cease to seek money they have not earned, will not confuse luxuries with necessities, will use God's goods

---

[98] St. Ambrose (c. 340-397), Bishop of Milan and Doctor.

with a reverence that will startle and give pause to others who live by "conspicuous consumption." One of the most powerful paradoxes of Christianity is this: that the truly poor person — not in the sense of destitution, which cries to Heaven for vengeance, but in the sense of a radical simplicity of life — is the wealthiest of all. The father in whom poverty of spirit is a living virtue finds himself richer and freer than anyone who is wealthy.

For the father of a family, who with his wife must make important decisions concerning money, this virtue in its fullness is particularly indispensable. Only when he has detached himself from things, only when he has detached himself even from the consideration of time as somehow his own property, will he be able to give fully. Then the giving will not only be easy; it will be a giving that finds him constantly replenished.

The man who, like St. Francis, considers nothing his own, but all things God's to be used for God's purposes, will find himself enormously rich: all of creation becomes his. Blessed are those who know they are poor.

Strive for detachment from possessions we must have

None of us can escape having. Not even the vowed religious can escape having clothes, books, and the tools necessary for work. But the vowed religious strives not to forget that what is used or worn is for the good of others. Such people strive to liberate themselves from the attachment to possessions that so easily drives a wedge between the heart and God. But one does not have to be a vowed religious to practice this virtue of spiritual poverty. In fact, even a wealthy person can be poor in spirit, although it is terribly difficult.

"And Jesus looked around and said to His disciples, 'How hard it will be for those who have wealth to enter the kingdom of God!'

And the disciples were amazed at His words."[99] The disciples' incredulity at Christ's pronouncement was similar to ours. Their question shows how well they understand what Jesus is saying. For few people can detach themselves spiritually from their possessions, so strong is the hold material things have on our affections.

"Jesus looked at them and said, 'With men it is impossible, but not with God.' "[100] It is, then, in response to the movement of God within us that we can achieve that necessary detachment. Even the very rich person may hear God's call, respond, and see the way clear to that self-denial which is fundamental to Christianity. "Poverty of spirit," says a classic work by Père Regamey on this subject, "is at once the first word and the last of supernatural life. It opens the Kingdom of Heaven to us, and the supreme action of Charity [love] is to become poor in God. Every stage of our progress is under the law of poverty."

Chastity allows sex the dignity God has given it

Another concern for any father is chastity, which means the right use of sex. No Christian can deny the need for genuine chastity in our society. Sexual immorality is so prevalent today that some think the term *immoral* applies only to sex! The contemporary insanity about sex is rooted not in an overestimation of sex — as one at first might be tempted to believe — but in a gross *undervaluation*, a degradation, of sex.

Some look upon sex as a toy they are lucky enough to have, something they can play with; others see it is a commodity to be sold or as a means of selling commodities; some confuse it with love, while others treat it as a dirty little secret.

[99] Mark 10:23-24.
[100] Mark 10:27.

All of these individuals, even those who see sex as the greatest motivation in people's lives, are defiling sex. They are refusing to grant to the sexual the goodness that God has given it. They will not honor sex for what it is: a deeply good gift of God to be used as a means for a more intimate love for one's spouse, for a more intimate union with God, and for God's greatest work of creation.

The member of a religious order or congregation who takes a vow of chastity chooses to use his sexuality in a celibate manner. Celibate chastity is not an excuse to avoid people or relate to others in a cold and distant way. Rather, it is a decision to love others in ways other than what marriage allows.

Chastity is for married people, too!

The father of a family is by definition a non-celibate, of course, but he must nonetheless be chaste. While he has been called to the married life, he is yet called upon to reverence and enjoy sex for what it is. His chastity consists of using his gift only within the marriage union, of recognizing in it not only a means of expressing his deepest commitment to another, and for co-creating new lives for God, but as one expression of his love for God, as indeed, the core of the "great mystery" that is the sacrament of marriage.

Chastity, then, is not, as some seem to believe, a mere negation of sexual immorality, but a positive respect for the goodness of sex. It is this awareness of the holiness of sex that will provide the father of the family with the resources whereby he can withstand and even help to counteract the distorters of sex who have stained the very atmosphere of daily life.

That high regard for sexual intercourse, along with that sense of its goodness and the goodness of its pleasure, is as essential to the married man as to the single, if either is to keep his mind and heart clean in a society where obscene and trivial notions of sex abound. Our fidelity to our wives must be a fidelity fixed firmly in a chaste mind, a chaste heart.

Our sex-saturated society makes chastity a challenge

Maintaining a healthy Christian attitude toward women can be difficult in our culture. The advertising industry, our entertainment media, and many magazines and books are overtly calculated to arouse adulterous thoughts in us and to encourage us to look at women as sexual objects.

To some it may seem strange to talk of discipline within marriage, but it is to be hoped that the Christian man still realizes that, even within marriage, he has need to discipline himself. Sexual intercourse should be truly an act of love; its meaning is reduced when it merely becomes a habit or a source of personal pleasure with little thought of the other person. On the other hand, at those times when abstinence from sexual intercourse is necessary, during the wife's menstrual period, for instance, that abstinence should be rooted in love, too.

The man who has mastery over his sexual powers, who has practiced restraint, is the man who will be capable of finding in those times of abstinence a deepening love for his wife. What could be a source of tension can be a spring out of which flows a deeper love.

Make time to make love

In our day, however, chances are that a man will find that he must make an equal effort to make love joyfully with his wife on a regular basis! Married couples typically find themselves so fatigued at the end of the day, and at the end of the week, that they fall into bed exhausted with little energy left for making love. Yet sexual intercourse is an important part of a marital spirituality, so it is critical that times be found to make love leisurely and with joy.

Head of the Family

The husband can take the lead in this by planning ahead, by setting aside times when he and his wife can be alone — the occasional weekend, for example, spent away from the children. Some couples make it a point regularly to turn off the TV after the children are in bed for the night; then they talk intimately and make love. It's important to be creative! For the good of your marriage, take the trouble to enjoy God's gift of sexual pleasure regularly.

God has given the father of the family a share in the enriching of the universe by bringing into it more love. If God praises and rewards the faithful servant for the fruitful use of his five talents, what praise, what reward, will God reserve for the father who has cherished his wife and, with her, raised up for God the human lives entrusted to them, lives worth more than all the gold and silver in the world?

In the end, the father of the family will become a real-world saint by being what he is called to be: faithful to his marriage in every respect, warm and reliable in his love for his children, and, in all that he does, a faith-filled channel of the love of his Father in Heaven, who, as St. Augustine said, is closer to him than he is to himself.

Biographical Note

Clayton C. Barbeau

C layton C. Barbeau is an internationally recognized family
therapist whose books, tapes, and lectures have helped
thousands to become better spouses, parents, and Christians.

He has been called "the poet of mental health," and his reputa-
tion as a dynamic and inspirational author and speaker has taken
him throughout the United States — and to twenty-six foreign
countries — to deliver a hopeful message of mental and spiritual
wholeness.

The father of eight children, Barbeau lives and runs a private
practice in San Francisco.

Sophia Institute Press®